T0295809

Mastering Facilitation

Mastering Facilitation

A Guide for Assisting Teams and Achieving Great Outcomes

By
Dr Morgan L Jones

A PRODUCTIVITY PRESS BOOK

First published 2021
by Routledge
600 Broken Sound Parkway #300, Boca Raton FL, 33487

and by Routledge
2 Park Square, Milton Park, Abingdon, Oxon, OX14 4RN

Routledge is an imprint of the Taylor & Francis Group, an informa business

© 2021 Taylor & Francis

ISBN: 9780367543464 (hbk)
ISBN: 9780367543457 (pbk)
ISBN: 9781003088868 (ebk)

Typeset in Minion Pro
by Deanta Global Publishing Services, Chennai, India

Contents

Preface xv
Acknowledgements xvii

SECTION I   Facilitation Fundamentals

Chapter 1   What Is Facilitation? 3

The Roles of a Facilitator 5
The Responsibilities of a Facilitator 8
Guiding Principles of Facilitation 11
  Equality 11
  Empathy 11
  Mutual Trust 11
  Focus 11
  Free and Informed Choice 12
  Shared Decision-Making 12
  Responsibility and Commitment 12
  Involvement by All 12
Chapter Summary 12

Chapter 2   Mastering Technique: The Facilitation Process............. 13

Planning Dimension 13
Meaning Dimension..14
Confronting Dimension 14
Feeling Dimension...15
Structuring Dimension..15
Valuing Dimension 15
Planning the Facilitation 16
  What Should You Know before You Plan the Agenda
  or the Facilitation Program?....................................17
    The Goals of the Facilitation and the Measures of
    Success 17

Manner of Facilitation..17
Group Composition..17
Available Information 17
Climate and Environment 18
Location..18
Logistics and Room Requirements.....................18
Equipment, Supplies and Materials....................19
Food and Refreshments..19
Before the Facilitation Sessions.............................. 20
Starting the Facilitation 22
Introduce Yourself..22
State the Reason for the Program or Session 22
Welcome and Acknowledge Everyone................22
Make Introductions..22
Set the Rules of Conversation 23
Identify Motives 26
Begin with a Punch...26
Starting with a Punch Line...................................26
Personal 27
Unexpected 27
Novel 27
Challenging...28
Humorous 29
During the Facilitation 30
What If the Group Resists Being Facilitated? 31
What If the Group Is Pressed for Time?.............31
What If the Team Is Going around in Circles?...................32
What If the Group Ignores Its Own Rules?........................32
Prevention 34
Non-Intervention..36
Low-Level Intervention 36
Medium-Level Intervention 38
High-Level Intervention 38
Step 1..38
Step 2..38
Step 3..38
Ending the Facilitation 40
After the Facilitation (Follow-up)............................. 42
Chapter Summary 43

SECTION II   Core Facilitation Skills

Chapter 3   Mastering Facilitation: Behavioural Techniques
in Facilitation 47

Core Values of Mastering Facilitation 48
Flexibility 48
Confidence 48
Authenticity 48
Integrity 48
Patience/Perseverance 49
Leadership (Presence) 49
Initiating 49
Perceptive 49
The Art of Listening 50
Synergistic Listening Is Deliberate 51
Synergistic Listening Is Empathetic 51
Synergistic Listening Is Multisensory 51
Synergistic Listening Is Active 51
Synergistic Listening Is a Learning Experience 52
Synergistic Listening Is Non-Judgemental 52
Synergistic Listening Is Dynamic 52
How the Master Facilitator Listens 53
Verbal Listening: Listening with Words 53
Non-Verbal Listening: Listening with Your Body 55
Do 55
Don't 55
Para-Verbal Listening: Listening with
Your Voice 55
Listening to the Group: Getting the Big Picture 56
The Art of Synergistic Questioning 58
Blooming Questions 59
Knowledge Level 60
Comprehension Level 60
Application Level 60
Analysis Level 61
Synthesis Level 61
Evaluation Level 61
Asking like Socrates 62

Throwing APPLES: What to Ask, When to Ask, How to Ask 65

    Affective Questions..67

    Managerial and Structuring Questions.............................67

    Rhetorical Questions...67

    Focusing/Refocusing Questions 68

    Open and Closed Questions... 68

Quick Tips in Questioning...70

The Ladder of Inference: A Framework for Making Minds Meet...71

    Lesson 1: Rule Your Mind or It Will Rule You 73

    Lesson 2: Stay as Low as You Can.....................................74

    Lesson 3: Learn to Swim before You Dive.........................74

    Lesson 4: When in Doubt, Check It Out 74

    Lesson 5: Avoid Simplification..74

    Lesson 6: Different Folks, Different Strokes......................74

Chapter Summary 76

Chapter 4   Conflict Resolution and Decision-Making 77

The Nature of Group Conflict..77

Conflict Resolution..79

    Strategic Responses to Conflict...81

        Competing Strategy...81

        Collaborating Strategy 81

Compromising Strategy..81

    Avoiding Strategy...82

    Accommodating Strategy 82

    Guidelines for Negotiation 82

        Benefits of Interest-Based Negotiation........................82

        Create Safety 83

        Facilitative Listening...84

        Feedback..84

        Reflection...84

    Attributes of Skilled Negotiators 84

    Consensus Decision-Making 85

        Conditions for Consensus...86

        Working Together 86

        Commitment to Reaching Consensus 86

Trust and Openness..87
Sufficient Time..87
Clear Process...87
Facilitation 87
Key Skills for Consensus.. 88
A Consensus Flowchart... 88
The Decision-Making Process.. 88
Guidelines for Reaching Consensus............................... 90
Agreement and Disagreement...91
Consensus in Large Groups..92
Chapter Summary 93

SECTION III   Advanced Facilitation Skills and Methods

Chapter 5   Understanding Groups and Individuals: Facilitating
a Synergistic Dynamic 97

Dimensions of Group Interactions and Relationships......... 99
Cycles of Group Development 102
Forming...104
Storming..104
Norming..104
Performing...105
Adjourning 105
Adult Learning Styles..106
Kolb's Learning Styles 106
Honey and Mumford's Learning Cycle 110
The Attention, Generation, Emotion and Spacing
(AGES) Model.. 116
Attention 117
Generation 118
Emotions 119
Spacing 120
Principles of Adult Learning..121
The "Four-Quadrant" Opening: Motivating the
Adult Learner 125
Levels of Focus 127
Vision...129

Aim 129
Challenges 129
Opportunities 129
Facilitator Focus 129
Planning 129
Aim 129
Challenges 129
Opportunities 130
Facilitator Focus 130
Details 130
Aim 130
Challenges 130
Opportunities 130
Facilitator Focus 130
Problems 131
Aim 131
Challenges 131
Opportunities 131
Facilitator Focus 131
Drama 131
Aim 131
Challenges 131
Opportunities 131
Facilitator Focus 132
The CARER Model 133
The CARER Model Explained 135
Certainty (Predictable) 135
Autonomy (Discretion) 136
Relatedness (Bonding) 137
Equity (Fairness) 138
Reputation (Status) 139
Dynamic CARER Domain Links 140
CARER and Facilitation 141
Conclusions 142
A Facilitative Approach to Learning 143
Types of Facilitation 143
The Neutral Facilitator 143
The Trainer as a Facilitator 143
Process versus Content 143

Organising "Brainstorming" Information: The ToP
Method 144
Pyramid Brainstorming...145
   Forced Comparison: Use of Sticky Dots......................146
   Process 146
Basic Tools...147
   Flipcharts 147
   Providing a "Group Memory"......................................147
   Facilitating the Process 147
   "Presentation" Skills: The Use of Colour and
   Graphics 147
Summarising and Paraphrasing...149
Paraphrasing and Clarifying...150
Questioning 150
   Multiple Learning Styles 151
Chapter Summary 152

Chapter 6 Special Facilitation Techniques...................................... 153

Facilitating Executive Teams 153
   Overall Approach and Attitude.................................... 154
   Establishing the Right Tone for the Session.................155
   Establishing Discussion Guidelines 156
   Strategic Alignment..156
   Maximise Your Executive Team's Capabilities 157
   Conclusion 158
Facilitating Change 159
   Change Management: The TFDS Model 159
Facilitating Virtual Teams 160
   Use Video..161
   Do a "Take 5"..161
   Assign Different Tasks 161
   Forbid the Use of the "Mute" Function 162
   Penalise Multitaskers...162
Facilitating Project Improvement..162
   Facilitation Skills for Today's Project Leaders 163
   Inspires a Shared Vision...163
   Good Communicator 163
   Integrity..164

Enthusiasm..164

Empathy 164

Competence 165

Ability to Delegate Tasks...............................165

Cool Under Pressure 165

Team-Building Skills 166

Problem-Solving Skills 166

Chapter Summary 166

SECTION IV   Evaluation and Conclusion

Chapter 7   Facilitation Skills Evaluation and Improvement.......... 169

The Six Megatrends 169

Facilitators We Dread...170

Vince Lombardi 170

The Drill Sergeant 170

The Guardian..170

The Know-It-All 170

The Ice Cube 170

The Blabber 171

The Pretender 171

The "I Can't Hear You" Guy 171

The Marathon Man...171

The Parrot 171

The Molasses Man 171

The Passenger 171

The Storyteller 171

The Centrepiece..171

The Tunnel Driver..172

Facilitation Skill Levels 172

Chinese proverb 172

Self-Assessment..173

Trust and Support..174

Communication 174

Making Group Decisions.................................174

Cooperating..175

Teamwork..175

Problem-Solving 175
Leadership Roles 176
Giving and Receiving Feedback 176
Respecting Personal Differences 176
Closure Questions 176
Participant Evaluation Template 177
Group Questionnaire 180
Questionnaire: "Burnout" 182
Questionnaire: "Session Feedback" 184
Presentation Indicators 184
Content Indicators 185
Impact Indicators 186
Chapter Summary 187

Chapter 8 Conclusion 189

Bibliography 191

Appendices 195
Appendix 1 Functions of a Facilitator 195
Create Collaborative Client Relationships 195
Plan Appropriate Group Processes 195
Create and Sustain a Participatory Environment 195
Guide Group to Appropriate and Useful Outcomes 195
Build and Maintain Professional Knowledge 195
Model Positive Professional Attitude 196
Appendix 2 List of Verbs for Constructing Learning
Outcomes and Questions* 196
Appendix 3 Session Scope 198
Appendix 4 Participant Evaluation Template 199
Appendix 5 Group Questionnaire 202
Appendix 6 Questionnaire: "Burnout" 204
Appendix 7 Questionnaire: "Session Feedback" 207
Presentation Indicators 207
Content Indicators 208
Impact Indicators 208
Appendix 8 Tips for Online Facilitating 209
Preparation 209

Index 215

Some of the proceeds from this book will be donated to Redkite, an Australian charity supporting children, teenagers and their families affected by cancer, directly or through a family member.

Redkite provides essential support to children, teenagers and young adults with cancer to ensure the best possible quality of life for them and their family – now and into the future. Every child and young person's experience of cancer is unique. To give a child or young person the best chance of managing the cancer journey positively, the whole family and each individual needs to be supported to manage their unique cancer experience. By alleviating the financial and emotional stress and enabling children, young people, their families and their support networks to develop their strengths and skills, Redkite assists the whole family to achieve that positive end.

Preface

WHY WRITE THIS BOOK?

With business and organisations moving at an ever-faster pace and facing more and more demanding challenges, the need for efficient, succinct and productive interaction between individuals of those businesses and organisations is more important than ever. With the bounds of communication restrictions abandoned through technological advances (we can now see and hear anyone across any manner of virtual platforms anywhere around the globe) and with a greater understanding of the underlying dynamics of human interaction, unprecedented pressure has been thrust upon the individual or individuals who, often, enable these dynamic interactions: *the facilitator*.

Many of us have, at one time or other, been responsible for a meeting – whether between a small number of individuals or an entire organisation of hundreds, or possibly thousands, of businessmen and women.

Or, perhaps, we've had to be the mediator in a family dispute closer to home or managed a discussion between two feuding friends or colleagues. One way or another, chances are all of us have been a *facilitator* at some point in our lives.

I felt the need to write this book because with the ever-growing demands placed on facilitators – myself included – I found it increasingly difficult to find a methodical, structured approach to facilitation. Rather than facilitating "on the fly", I wanted to create a definitive guide to instruct and assist facilitators – both new and experienced – with a set of guidelines and underlying theory that will benefit any facilitator, whether as a mediator between two individuals, single-handedly facilitating a group of 100 or working as part of a facilitation team in a multinational corporation.

WHO SHOULD READ THIS BOOK?

A facilitator can be any individual (or individuals) who "facilitates" the interaction between two or more people – whether in a business, an organisation or otherwise. To that end, the advice, tools and explanations in this book will be a valuable opportunity for most people to gain an insight into structured facilitation. This book will be of particular value for the following:

- Managers and supervisors.
- Executive directors and board members.
- Facilitators, trainers and consultants.
- Educators.
- Active citizens and community workers.
- Attorneys.
- Marketers.
- Salespeople.
- Coaches and mentors.
- International business executives.
- Federal, state and local government employees.

Dr Morgan L Jones

Acknowledgements

I would like to acknowledge Kristen Hansen, Graeme Gherashe, John Ferrier, Vanessa Sewell-Rosenberg, Ben Reeve, Janeece Keller, Jon Pratlett, Johnny Young, Edwin Boyce, George Lee Sye and David Masters for their valuable comments and feedback on the manuscript. A special thank you goes to Ashley Cooper for transforming our drafts into professional figures throughout the book. Special thanks also to the many people who have attended my courses and been facilitated by me over the years and those facilitators that I have had the privilege to observe and work with.

Section I

Facilitation Fundamentals

1

What Is Facilitation?

What we call leadership consists mainly of knowing how to follow. The wise leader stays in the background and facilitates other people's process.

When two or more people meet, it is almost certain that there will be some degree of conflict. In working groups, where the members come from diverse backgrounds, characteristics, interests and abilities, different opinions are inevitable and normal. Ideas collide. Personalities clash. Motives and interests wrestle with the greater good. The direction of the group goes astray, the goals of the meeting are sidelined and organisational objectives deserted. Not that conflict is all bad because agreements borne from disagreements are sometimes the most novel yet most valuable.

In the workplace, such as during organisational or strategic planning, decision-making, project development and training sessions, there must be somebody, and not just anybody, to provide opportunities for synergy and productive interaction to enable the participants to work effectively and achieve the purpose(s) of the group. This somebody is the facilitator.

To facilitate simply means "to make easy". To facilitate means to make it easier for a group to move from the starting point to the desired end by managing the journey, helping the group maintain focus and move forwards. The focus of this book is facilitating groups. As a facilitator, your job is to guide and manage the group through processes or methods to reach the goals as agreed. You are concerned with *how* decisions are reached, rather than with what decisions are made. You are not concerned with what is being discussed, but with how the discussion proceeds; not with what the problem is, but with how the group arrives at a solution or outcome. You are not there to solve their problems, but to provide the guidance necessary to help *them* solve their problems. You are not there to think for them, but to help them think for themselves. The facilitator focuses on the means and not the end, on the process rather than the content.

A facilitator is different from a team leader and project manager, although there may be occasions when an individual takes on these three roles. To distinguish, the leader envisions the future and sets the target or direction, the manager sets out the plans and activities to accomplish the vision and the facilitator focuses on the group processes (in a neutral manner) to achieve project success. But through their skilled facilitation of group processes and interactions, the facilitator in effect "leads" and "manages" the group to achieve its purposes.

As described by Schwarz (2005), the group facilitator is someone whose selection is acceptable to all members of the group, who is substantively neutral, has no substantive decision-making authority and, by means of a guided process and structure, he or she can effectively assist the group in identifying and solving problems or can assist in making decisions.

The main points of Schwarz's definition are:

- The facilitator is a third party – separate and distinct from the group, but he is accepted by the members.
- The facilitator is neutral. (The paradox is that the facilitator may not take sides but should intervene when the situation so warrants by making suggestions, which, in a way, could be seen as taking sides.) For example, the facilitator is often the Chairperson or the Team Leader and is, therefore, prone to not being automatically neutral. The skill of being a facilitator is to hold in check their own views in order to facilitate the group's ultimate outcomes – or to be honest and be willing to state where their own views lie. By placing their cards on the table, they can then let go of those views to facilitate.
- The facilitator is not the decision-making authority (otherwise, when the members realise that their actions and decisions could be disregarded or flouted by the facilitator, they will most probably be uninterested, unconcerned and uncommitted).
- The facilitator is concerned with process and structure to help the participants to focus on the task at hand and work successfully.

The facilitator has no formal power but has quiet authority. He or she does not dominate with their expertise, but stealthily commands the group. Facilitation should be like walking on rice paper – everyone knows you're present and yet you leave no footprints of any kind. People don't see the process (the footprints), but they still see you as the facilitator.

Although it is auspicious to have an external facilitator in many circumstances, there are times when you, as a leader, do not have the luxury of only leading or managing or championing a project. So, you take on the hats of leader, manager and facilitator. It is with an astute understanding of the nature of a problem or issue to be resolved that you get to decide which hat to put on – and when.

Remaining neutral is challenging for the facilitator because it requires him or her to manage the process of decision-making *without* influencing the decisions of the group. The facilitator must keep their knowledge, ideas, opinions and judgements to themselves. The facilitator cannot be biased about their method and techniques. Although flexible and adaptable, the facilitator decides and chooses which facilitation strategies and tools to utilise.

The skilled facilitator chooses which tools and behavioural techniques will develop individual skills and knowledge, create team synergy, optimise effectiveness and reap higher buy-in and commitment. They draw upon knowledge of group dynamics and learning styles as well as intuitive experience to be able to design the most synergistic facilitation strategy.

THE ROLES OF A FACILITATOR

Henry Kissinger once said, "The task of the leader is to get his people from where they are to where they have not been." Building on this, the task of the facilitator is to get people to where they want to be.

In today's organisations, the involvement of members of the different tiers are sought in decision-making and project implementation. The services of a facilitator are extremely useful in enabling diverse sets of workers to coordinate and harmonise their efforts. A facilitator is engaged for different purposes that span the different levels of the organisation.

These are some of the areas where the intervention of a facilitator is found to be extremely useful:

- Team building.
- Decision-making and problem-solving.
- Project conceptualisation/launching.
- Strategic planning.
- Research.
- Culture change or change management.

- Negotiation and conflict resolution.
- Team diagnostics.

Facilitators are usually invited to oversee a diverse range of organisational activities and sessions. For example:

- Planning and prioritisation of strategic options.
- Design and facilitation of dialogue.
- Gaining consensus on complex, cross-functional issues.
- Gathering perspectives from different organisational levels.
- Setting up new projects or jump-starting stalled ones.
- Identification of work problems.
- Breaking through team roadblocks.
- Facilitation of virtual teams/executive teams.
- Getting buy-in.
- Process checking.

Depending on the needs of the client, the facilitator may work alone, work with a co-facilitator or deliver training/learning jointly with organisational members. Facilitated activities could be one-shot only, take a few days or may be ongoing until the goal is achieved. A facilitator could be engaged to deal with one skill or topic or a wide-ranging set of subjects and skill areas (Figure 1.1).

Facilitation entails different degrees of knowledge, skill and involvement depending on the particular needs and purposes of a group. At times, an organisation may require your services as a consultant, trainer, coach, teacher or a pure facilitator. For some, pure facilitation is different from facilitative coaching, facilitative training, facilitative leadership and facilitative consultation, among others. For others, the facilitator's role has acquired new dimensions and modifications as trends in organisational leadership and management have also evolved.

The following are some of the most common mutations of facilitator roles with a description of their knowledge, team involvement and association, as defined by Schwarz (2002) (Table 1.1).

Except for neutrality, degree of influence in content decision-making and association with the group or client being facilitated, these roles observe the same basic principles and invariably utilise similar interactive approaches.

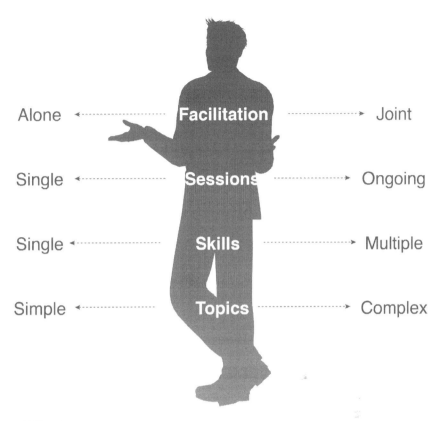

FIGURE 1.1
Types of facilitator engagement.

TABLE 1.1

Types of Facilitator Roles

Role	Association	Process expertise	Content expertise	Involvement
Facilitator	Third party	Process expert	Content neutral	Process only
Facilitative consultant	Third party	Process expert	Content expert	May be involved in content decision-making
Facilitative coach	Third party or group member	Process expert	Content expert	Involved in content decision-making
Facilitative trainer	Third party or group member	Process expert	Content expert	Involved in content decision-making
Facilitative leader	Team leader or member	Skilled	Involved in content	Involved in content decision-making

THE RESPONSIBILITIES OF A FACILITATOR

I believe this to be the mantra of the facilitator: Let it happen. Faced with a group that wants to cross the seven seas, let them build their vessels; a group that seeks to become self-sufficient, let them learn how to catch fish; a group that wants to reach the peak of success, let them make and climb the ladder to success.

The facilitator takes on multi-faceted functions and responsibilities in order to help a group achieve their purposes. As a methodical leader or a steward of the process, the facilitator paves a clear process and structure to tap the full potential of the group. Ultimately, the facilitator is a synergist.

Synergy comes from the Greek word *sunergia* meaning cooperation or working together. There is synergy when the result is greater than the sum of the parts. In a group of people, synergy is created when the combined effort of the members is greater than the sum of the individual efforts.

As a synergist, the facilitator has to focus on many dimensions of the group activity. He or she is a strategist, a guide, a collaborator, a peacemaker, a taskmaster, a trouble-shooter, a motivator and so on.

Building from the core values and facilitator functions set forth by the International Association of Facilitators (IAF), there are six basic roles the skilled facilitator should perform to be a complete synergist:

As a partner, the facilitator coordinates with both the client (organisation) and the group members to:

- Determine existing conditions and needs.
- Clarify assumptions, roles and expectations.
- Identify any possible conflicts of interests, challenges and issues.
- Set the goals of the group activity.
- Agree on the outcomes.

As a strategist, the facilitator designs a facilitation framework that will:

- Include tools and techniques suitable to the needs and objectives of the client and the group.
- Optimise client resources.
- Adjust group activities and structure as needed (Figure 1.2).

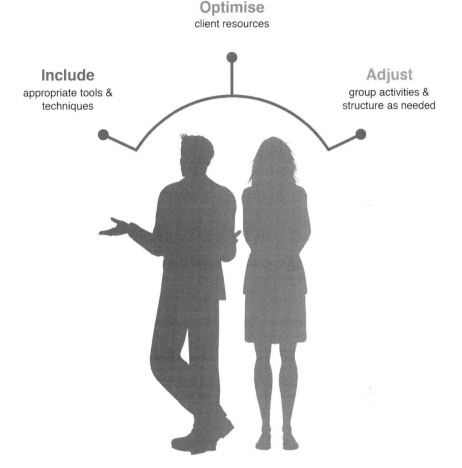

Optimise
client resources

Include
appropriate tools &
techniques

Adjust
group activities &
structure as needed

FIGURE 1.2
The facilitator as a strategist.

As a guide, the facilitator implements the facilitation plan to:

- Steer the group with effective tools and processes.
- Provide structure to group activities.
- Help reconcile a diverging direction with original intent.

As a peacemaker, the facilitator:

- Recognises the welfare and dignity of the participants.
- Creates a safe, peaceful and comfortable environment for the group.
- Resolves group and individual conflicts.
- Encourages democratic decision-making and consensus.

As a taskmaster, the facilitator:

- Keeps group activity on track, on focus and with momentum.
- Monitors time and schedule.
- Adapts to changing circumstances.
- Brings appropriate closure to the activity.

As a motivator, the facilitator must have the skills to:

- Draw out creative efforts and insights.
- Acknowledge input, productivity and progress.
- Encourage democratic and inclusive participation.
- Build commitment to the outcome.

This list is not exhaustive. There are many more functions and responsibilities that may be added, but these are the most crucial tasks of a facilitator.

In the context of modern organisations where traditional modes of doing things have changed drastically, organisational transformation has impacted on all tiers and dimensions.

Facilitators have been called to perform functions beyond their traditional roles of formulating sound agendas and managing meetings or training sessions. To that end, a skilled facilitator should strive to master a broader set of skills, knowledge and values to handle such emerging and challenging roles.

Learning point: Be clear of your role and responsibility as a facilitator. Avoid dual roles and role conflict.

- This was early in my career as a facilitator.
- I was asked to attend a very important global workshop as a participant with a view to contributing based on my functional knowledge. The workshop would be attended by six separate teams, each working on a separate well-defined topic.
- The workshop was to be held overseas and was of one week's duration.
- Just before departing, I was asked to also facilitate the team of which I was a member during the workshop.

- This proved to be extremely challenging due to the "conflict" that arose between my roles as "expert contributor" and "facilitator" on many occasions.
- It proved incredibly difficult to facilitate the group when I also had to actively contribute to the content of the discussion and influence the direction and outcome, as opposed to solely focusing on process and facilitation.
- At the end of the workshop, the team did achieve a very good outcome, but along the way, I recall feeling totally exhausted on more than one occasion and having a migraine along the way as well!

GUIDING PRINCIPLES OF FACILITATION

What principles should govern facilitation? What do we want to see in facilitated groups? The experts have different phraseologies for the most essential principles they believe should be present in facilitation, but these are the common themes that emerge:

Equality

Participants treat each other as equals. Equal opportunity and democratic participation are encouraged.

Empathy

Participants are encouraged to show compassion and understanding of the ideas and experiences of others. There is a sincere effort to listen to words and also to feelings.

Mutual Trust

Participants have confidence in each other and in each other's abilities. Doubt or scepticism about the motivations of other group members is replaced by respect.

Focus

The group is goal-oriented and all actions and decisions are directed towards success with passion and enthusiasm.

Free and Informed Choice

Participants set their objectives and choose the manner of achieving these purposes. Coercion and manipulation are forbidden.

Shared Decision-Making

There is an unrelenting pursuit to reach mutual agreements. Issues are discussed thoroughly and decisions are reached by consensus.

Responsibility and Commitment

Participants own their decision and feel totally responsible for it. There is an intrinsic commitment to action.

Involvement by All

All participants, regardless of their status, agenda, personality and so forth, are encouraged to involve themselves in the facilitation.

CHAPTER SUMMARY

The key points of this chapter are to understand:

- What facilitation is and what it is not, and what should be the expected outcomes of a facilitated session
- The role of a facilitator and situations of when to use an external facilitator and when as a leader you should facilitate
- There are different types of facilitator for different situations and the key focus areas for each situation.
- The key principles of facilitation independent of the situation and role they need to play.

2

Mastering Technique:
The Facilitation Process

There is no set recipe for how to facilitate groups. Every facilitative experience is to be treated as *sui generis*. No two groups are ever alike, mainly because they are composed of different sets of individuals who have varying experiences, skills and values. Even if groups consist of the same people, their purpose in every facilitated activity often varies. Even the same group, on the same topic, can react differently at different meetings according to the demands, stresses, etc. that may be impacting on them at a given point in time. Every approach must then be adaptive to variances of all these factors. This begs the question, "Should the facilitator then make a plan?"

The answer is, *yes*. One cannot sail the seven seas without a map. As experienced facilitators would assert, every group is a group in turbulence, to different degrees, palpable or not.

There are several aspects of the facilitation process that one needs to address when drawing the map. These are the six dimensions of facilitation: planning, meaning, confronting, feeling, structuring and valuing. The facilitator should consider all six dimensions when designing the facilitation process (Heron, 1999). For every dimension, a planner focuses on a key facilitative question (Figure 2.1).

PLANNING DIMENSION

The goal-oriented aspect of facilitation that hinges on the group's purpose.

- Question: *How shall the group achieve its objectives?*

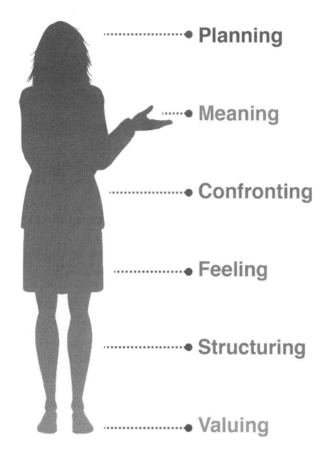

FIGURE 2.1
Dimensions of facilitation.

MEANING DIMENSION

The cognitive aspect that deals with participants' understanding of experience and the reason for their behaviours.

- Question: *How shall meaning be given to and found in the experiences and actions of group members?*

CONFRONTING DIMENSION

The challenge aspect which deals with raising consciousness about the group's reaction to things it needs to deal with.

- Question: *How shall the group's consciousness be raised about these matters?*

FEELING DIMENSION

The sensitive aspect which deals with the management of feelings and emotions within the group.

- Question: *How shall the life of feeling and emotion within the group be handled?*

STRUCTURING DIMENSION

The formal aspect of facilitation that has to do with methods of learning.

- Question: *How can learning be structured?*

VALUING DIMENSION

The integrity aspect of facilitation that honours and celebrates individual differences and needs and celebrates the group's collective wisdom.

- Question: *How can such a climate of personal value, integrity and respect be created?*

All these dimensions are acutely interrelated and are explained in different sections of this book. Suffice to say that, in setting up the facilitative process, facilitators need to start not with what they believe is important, but with the perspective of the group. It should be an inverted process of consideration. In other words, the facilitator asks, "If I were a participant, what would I want to see, learn and experience?" Facilitators should then look at the process, not from where *they* are, but from where the group is. It may also be advantageous to seek inputs from some of the group members in advance. Especially the ones who might prove to be awkward.

Sometimes, however, facilitators are faced with instances where a plan needs to be modified and, perhaps, even totally abandoned in extreme cases. Does it mean that the facilitator has to have a plan B or even a plan C? I believe, no. The facilitator has to be flexible and creative, drawing out intuitively from experience to improvise and respond to the moment, introducing some quick changes at great speed and flexibility. Another question is: should the facilitator go with the flow at all times? The answer is still, no. Facilitators should not be compelled to yield to whimsical and/or trivial desires of the group, most especially when the purpose of the group is thrust aside. By failing to do this, facilitators are absconding from their role. It is their responsibility to draw the group back to its original intent. However, facilitators should be astute enough to identify possibilities from deviance, especially when there is an opportunity for the group to flourish and surpass expectations. Surrendering does not mean yielding to the group, *per se*, but yielding to what is best for the group – that is, "going with the energy" if the energy is helping take the group in a sensible, potentially valuable direction.

PLANNING THE FACILITATION

In one of my researches, I encountered the following comment, told to me by a person who was attending the meeting: "I'm in a staff meeting. There are 83 ceiling tiles in our meeting room. And eight light fixtures, with 24 fluorescent bulbs. That is all." Imagine if the people you are facilitating were counting the number of times you blink or the number of participants wearing blue or the minutes left before you call for a break. Or perhaps spending all their analytical thinking on why there are only 83 ceiling tiles – which seems unsymmetrical, in any event. This was clearly a session that was ill-prepared and poorly managed.

Like a good soldier, the facilitator does not go into battle unprepared. After agreeing and contracting to facilitate, the facilitator prepares and outlines the facilitation process from beginning to middle to its end. In order to do this, you have to do a lot of pre-work. Know the *whys*, the *whats*, the *wheres* and the *whos*, before you can develop the facilitation plan (the *how*).

What Should You Know before You Plan the Agenda or the Facilitation Program?

The Goals of the Facilitation and the Measures of Success

The most important thing you should answer is *why* facilitate? You should agree with the client about the outcome that they need – what they want to see in the end to agree that the goal was achieved. Be clear about the specific success indicators. Make sure that the objective is clear and doable and within your capabilities. The way to do this is to start the goal statement with an action word.

After agreeing on the purpose of facilitation, you can then craft subobjectives to manage the process better.

Manner of Facilitation

Are you going to work alone? Or will the facilitation be a joint undertaking with organic members of the organisation? Depending on the nature of the activity, you will also need to decide whether you will need a co-facilitator.

Group Composition

Who is attending? What are their roles and functions? What are their skills, knowledge and values? Their experience? Their expectations? In large groups, it would not be feasible to know each individual's personality. What the facilitator does is interview group members from different organisational levels and functional units. You do not have to know everything, but at least enough that you can then be able to gauge their mindset and expectations and anticipate the intensity and direction of group dynamics. In cases where the overall purpose of the facilitation is to resolve conflicts, having prior knowledge of the group composition and their history is a must.

Available Information

What is known about the problem or situation? For example, if it is a project improvement activity, on what stage is the project team currently working? You don't have to personally meet people from the organisation to get the required data. You only need to pick up the phone and interview key members of the group or have the client send you relevant materials and information.

Climate and Environment

After knowing the *what*, the next question is the *where*. The success of facilitation is largely dependent on the climate and environment. It should be conducive to learning and group interaction. We loathe dining in dirty restaurants. We cringe in a cramped coach. We dread walking in a dark alley. An environment that is clean, orderly, well-lit and spacious is learner friendly. The setting is one of the first things (if not *the* first) that participants encounter. Let the venue be a nice welcome for everyone. What factors should you consider?

Location

The venue should be a place where the members will feel comfortable to engage. Key questions you would ask yourself as a facilitator include:

- Is it safe?
- Is it accessible?
- Does it have provisions for persons with disabilities?

By "safe venue" I don't mean safety from danger alone. It also means that the participants will not feel threatened to engage. This is especially true in conflict-habituated groups. The best thing to do is to find a "neutral" place. It must not be the territory of either side.

Logistics and Room Requirements

Check room space, acoustics, ventilation and lighting. Room size should be appropriate to group size. Furniture must be available for everyone to sit and work on. Room arrangement should enhance maximum participation and invite an air of conversation. Round table arrangement infuses a sense of equality and trust, as opposed to a formal lecture style arrangement, which makes members feel intimidated and detached. When the participants can engage face to face, there is more genuineness and understanding.

Equipment, Supplies and Materials

Are all the necessary facilitation aids ready? Do you have enough chart paper, index cards, post-its, sticker dots, cue cards, posters, chalkboards or whiteboards, markers and pens? Is the equipment working properly? Do you have readily accessible materials such as stories, ideas, questions, concepts, expectations, ground rules, jokes, icebreakers, energisers and so on?

Food and Refreshments

One of the barriers to group productivity is discomfort. Grumbling stomachs will affect focus. Make sure there is enough provision for coffee and tea, food and snacks. I find that when people have coffee or tea during meetings, the climate becomes informal and less tense, and the discussions become more conversational.

Once you have considered all the logistics, you can begin to formulate your plan based on the dimensions of facilitation. After finishing the plan, the preparation is not yet done. It always pays to rehearse (not memorise the script). Conduct a dry run with peers or with a mentor or a coach. Have someone listen to you as you go through your plan, keeping yourself open to criticisms. Baring your plan to peers has many benefits. You are able to anticipate problems, you can relieve some of the nervousness in the presentation and you can also spare yourself from future embarrassment by rectifying any flaws. End the dry run with a peer review and then incorporate feedback and suggestions to improve the facilitation structure. Lastly, make periodic, mental rehearsals of the proceedings to commit them to memory.

Lastly, don't forget to send out the agenda to the participants. Include notification, reminders, handouts, notes and other reading materials, if any. Aside from giving them the opportunity to learn in advance, you are also showing them that you have prepared for them.

There are many benefits of adequate preparation, the first of which is that it gives you confidence. When you know your plan by heart, all you need to do is execute it, purposefully and confidently. This will communicate to the learners that you are in control and this translates into credibility. If you lack preparation, you will surely trip along the way. You will be uneasy and unsure. The audience will sense your unpreparedness and may withdraw or feel uncomfortable. As the prolific conductor and composer

André Previn said, "If I miss a day of practice, I know it. If I miss two days, my manager knows it. If I miss three days, my audience knows it." Preparation infuses a kind of magic in your execution because it translates to looking spontaneous, natural and genuine.

Before the Facilitation Sessions

Facilitation begins the moment a group agrees to meet and have a discussion, whether it be a weekly meeting, a project team update or a report to the Board of Directors. All participants begin to respond to the meeting request, agenda or report by, at the very least, putting it into their diary or gathering notes for it. People will come with many different agendas. Some are transparent – some not. Views will already have been formed by the participants in many instances, including any issues they want to be tabled, as well as issues they do *not* want to be tabled.

A couple of hours before the actual session begins, there are some things you need to do to establish the mood.

Be punctual. Be there when the participants start to arrive. A warm smile or a warm welcome helps greatly in setting the mood. Being early also allows you to do some last-minute checks of the venue.

Check if all equipment and tools are working well. Everyone hates a malfunctioning microphone or a laptop that takes aeons to boot up. Check if all supplies and logistics, including food and refreshments, are ready.

Have some key materials, like bulleted lists or drawings (except those that you wish to introduce with an element of surprise) posted in key areas so that the participants can start browsing them and get an idea of what's in store for them. Again, these all translate to perceptual readiness and the participants will appreciate that.

It's easier to socialise earlier on, as the participants are more likely to be by themselves. Have a chat with the early arrivals. Introduce yourself. Ask their names and a little bit of information. Share a joke. Exchange pleasantries. Implicitly give them the message that you are all equals and that you're genuinely interested in them. This demonstrates that you are relaxed and happy to be there. Indeed, you can use bits and pieces of the information you learn in your actual presentation. In this sense, facilitation starts well before you have even formally opened.

Moreover, the early interaction helps the facilitator to dynamically connect to the group by engaging with them on an interpersonal level (sometimes, with members one-on-one), in addition to the professional connection. By demonstrating his or her "human side", the facilitator not only builds trust, but also builds a safe environment for the group and facilitates the participants – both individually and as a collective – to feel more at ease about opening up.

Lastly, and importantly, start the meeting on time. Don't let the participants think that you have wasted a few minutes of their time. Those who come on time feel cheated that they rushed to get there.

In Chapter 5, I discuss the "Certainty, Autonomy, Relatedness, Equity and Reputation (CARER)" model. The advanced CARER group dynamic model will greatly enhance your understanding of group interaction at every level of facilitation.

Learning point: Learn who the influencers are in the group and as you prepare to facilitate the session(s), don't be afraid to use such people as a "sounding board" in advance.

- I was facilitator for quarterly meetings of a global peer group of senior operations and technology directors.
- I had a good relationship with the leader of the peer group. He was influential, but the others on the peer group did not report directly to him. So he couldn't simply instruct them what to do.
- The first couple of meetings went well, but I felt they could have gone even better. The facilitation process I had designed worked well, but it was taking a wee bit longer than necessary as one of the other more experienced and influential guys on the team was regularly commenting on/asking questions about the process before accepting it fully, contributing and being ready to move on.
- He never disagreed with it, just seemed to need to confirm his understanding of it and agreement with it as we moved along.
- This was using up valuable time and becoming mildly frustrating for some of the others.
- So, in advance of the remaining meetings, I asked him if he'd mind me using him as a "sounding board" after I had reviewed the agenda and designed the facilitation process for each meeting.
- I walked him through my proposed process on each occasion and 90% of the time I ended up making no changes.
- He was delighted with this type of involvement and things worked exceedingly well and smoothly from then onwards.

STARTING THE FACILITATION

This is one part of the activity that the facilitator has to plan well. Middles and endings almost always depend on the beginning. Continuing the cliché, the journey begins with one single step. To continue with the metaphor, the next thing to do is get everyone on board before setting sail. The first part of the activity should set the tone and clarify the direction of the group and get them involved. Here's what the facilitator has to do at the start of the process:

Introduce Yourself

In not more than 30 seconds, tell them something about yourself. Don't give a biographical narrative. Don't let them think, "So now, this meeting is about you. Why should I care?"

State the Reason for the Program or Session

Establish focus right at the start by stating, in no uncertain terms, the reason why everyone is there. Just state the general purpose without going into the detailed objectives. Do not give a history of a problem or issue lest you risk being perceived as biased. Avoid letting the participants think, "What do you know? I work here, I live here. I encounter that problem every day." It's their job to define the problem later.

Welcome and Acknowledge Everyone

Thank them for coming. If it is a big group, you could acknowledge them by calling out their affiliations.

Make Introductions

Even in groups where the participants are familiar with each other, you still have to let them introduce themselves. There is no set way to do this. It depends upon the size of the group and the nature of its purpose. Instead of just stating their name and position, you may ask them to briefly answer a question related to the group's purpose in two to three sentences.

In this way, you are able to gather useful information right at the start, perhaps about their inclinations or their attitudes. However, be careful about being judgemental.

Examples of introductions:

- *I am ... My leadership style is _____. I want to improve the way I ...*
- *I am ... I work well with ... but I find it difficult to work with ...*
- *I am ... They say I am ... but I am really ...*
- *I am ... I love to ... but I dislike ...*
- *I am ... I got involved with the organisation because ...*

Another method of introductions is to let the members say their names and their answer to the question to the person to their right, who will then do the introduction by saying something like, "In meeting John, I believe I have discovered that he believes that when we all think alike, no one is thinking at all. Hence, there's no creativity. He plays cricket and loves to go fishing."

Consider these other conversation starters:

- *The most inspiring leader to me is ... because ...*
- *My favourite letter (or number) is ... because ...*
- *The best measure of success is ...*
- *The most challenging task I ever encountered in my job was ...*
- *Employees are most creative when ...*
- *Nothing is as frustrating as ...*
- *When I have something to say, I ...*
- *The best teacher I ever had ...*

Set the Rules of Conversation

They are often termed as "ground rules", but referring to them as rules of conversation (or dialogue or engagement) also helps in reminding the participants that everyone is there to talk or to dialogue or to engage with each other and not to compete. The important thing, however, is that the rules must be set and agreed to by the whole group. They will conclude, "Hey, he is giving us the reins to police ourselves. He doesn't dictate to us what we can do and what we can't."

Some rules that enhance the facilitation process are:

Do:

- Wait for your turn to speak.
- Raise your hand if you have something to say.
- Listen sincerely.
- Evaluate the idea, not the person.
- Respect each other as equals.
- Treat all ideas as valid.
- Praise good work.
- Keep these rules.

Don't:

- Mock or attack other people's ideas.
- Talk too long.
- Keep others waiting for you.
- Shout at each other.
- Be late in coming to sessions.
- Answer mobile phones in the room.

If you think there is something important but missing on the board, you may give a suggestion, but not directly. Say something like, "What do we do if somebody keeps asking the same question?" Or, "What do we do if two people are talking at the same time?" It is important that you "check in" with the group before you write up an idea on the board. Get their agreement and have them say, "Yes!" out loud. Then, have these rules posted in key places, because you may have to refer to them from time to time.

Some groups also include hand signals or gestures in their ground rules. Using gestures instead of spoken words saves a lot of time and, in many instances, shows the facilitator's emerging dynamics. Instead of saying, "I just like to add that I am in complete agreement with …", the participant will only have to give a silent applause using hands. Hand signals are useful in large groups or in multilingual groups (Figure 2.2).

Although using hand gestures has advantages, it also has some downsides, especially if they are abused. The facilitator still has to police the participants. Dominators or majority groups will still try to dominate or monopolise. The facilitator has to ensure that the silent minority – or

Thumbs up or wiggling of fingers on both hands – to indicate agreement.

Thumbs down or raising the fist – to indicate a block or disagreement.

Thumbs sideways – divided feelings (having concerns but won't block decision).

Raising one hand – a desire to contribute to the discussion with a general point.

Raising both hands or pointing index finger up – point of information (to directly respond to the current discussion).

T-shape with both hands or triangle-shape with both hands – point of order or point of process.

Fist-to-Five:
- Fist – disagreement.
- One finger – to suggest changes.
- Two fingers – to discuss minor issues.
- Three fingers – to indicate willingness to let issue pass without further discussion.
- Four fingers – to indicate full agreement.
- Five fingers – to volunteer to take a lead in implementing the decision.

C-shape – to shoot a clarifying question.

FIGURE 2.2
Useful hand gestures.

the marginalised voices – are encouraged to participate. Make sure that hand signals give the participants an opportunity to participate, not the opportunity to speak.

Overuse of gestures may also make the session look like a pantomime. The facilitator should always be on guard when the overuse of these tools leads the focus further away from the purpose.

Identify Motives

An overarching view of what each individual's motives are will be an advantage later in the facilitation – or when things go wrong. The exercise "Explorer, Shopper, Vacationer and Prisoner" is a great way to find out who is in the room.

In this exercise, ask the group the following questions and ask each individual to raise their hand in response:

- *Who is here to really dive in, extract the juice and to embrace the journey with a sense of adventure?* **(Explorers)**
- *Who is here to have a look and find at least one great idea they can take away with them?* **(Shoppers)**
- *Who is here so they can have a break from their day-to-day grind?* **(Vacationers)**
- *Who is here because they have to be?* **(Prisoners)**

Begin with a Punch

There's no set way of introducing material to perk up conversations. You may start with a video clip or a powerful story or a punchy quotation, and then assemble the participants in pairs or small groups to answer questions about the material just presented to them. The rule is that the opening should catch interest and excitement.

Starting with a Punch Line

According to Garr Reynolds, there are five elements to observe in starting a presentation, and they are encapsulated in the acronym PUNCH:

- Personal.
- Unexpected.

- **Novel.**
- **Challenging.**
- **Humorous.**

Personal

Make your opening personal, but relevant. The material may not be necessarily about you, but including a bit of your experience demonstrates that you are opening up to the participants, in a way, getting personal with them. You may also use a real-life story that appeals to humanity. It should be poignant, such that it touches their hearts.

For example, you can use the documentary *Life without Pain* (2005) where Melody Gilbert tells the story of nine-year-old Gabby Gingras who is like every other child around her, except that she cannot feel pain, cold or heat. She suffers from a rare disease known as CIPA (congenital insensitivity to pain with anhidrosis), of which only 100 cases have been documented around the world. She has lost one eye because of over-scratching and keeps wounding herself. Then, you can ask the audience if they wished to be like Gabby, insensitive to pain, yet devoid of a basic defence mechanism. This story could work well in different types of activities such as team-building or self-awareness sessions.

Unexpected

Something that has an element of surprise or perhaps a story that is inconsistent with common beliefs (and which is relevant to the current task) would be an effective opening. For instance, if the session was on team-building or for creativity and innovation, you could use a quote that was unexpected from that person. Take these examples: Robert Millikan, recipient of the 1923 Nobel Prize in Physics, said, "There is no likelihood man can ever tap the power of the atom." Or Western Union, when the company said, "What use could the company make of an electric toy?" in relation to it turning down the rights to the telephone in 1878.

Novel

You may also opt to give them a scenario that appeals to their sense of wonder and for the unknown. It may be something extraordinarily unique, such that it stimulates them to look at an issue from another angle.

Or perhaps you can show them The Pale Blue Dot, the iconic image taken by NASA's Voyager 1 spacecraft from a distance of almost 4 billion miles from earth. Ask the participants to spot where the earth is (it is the dot about halfway down the orange stripe on the right), or better yet, let them guess what the image is.

Carl Sagan, who requested that NASA turn the spacecraft around in 1990 to take the image across the greatest extent of space yet travelled, in writing about this dot said:

> everyone you love, everyone you know, everyone you ever heard of, every human being who ever was, lived out their lives. The aggregate of our joy and suffering, thousands of confident religions, ideologies, and economic doctrines, every hunter and forager, every hero and coward, every creator and destroyer of civilization, every king and peasant, every young couple in love, every mother and father, hopeful child, inventor and explorer, every teacher of morals, every corrupt politician, every "superstar," every "supreme leader," every saint and sinner in the history of our species lived there – on a mote of dust suspended in a sunbeam.

Challenging

When people are challenged, they react almost instantly. You can tap the potential of thought-provoking material to stimulate imagination, interest, curiosity and excitement in the participants. Use material that challenges norms, practices and commonly held beliefs or that even defies logic. For example, ask them if they believe in levitation. Then, ask them if inanimate objects could have the ability to levitate. Finally, tell them the story about Japan's future transportation marvel – a floating Maglev train, designed to hit 311 miles per hour.

The prototype is a 92-foot-long front car with a lengthy aerodynamic nose and a 14-carriage train that floats above the tracks. Through magnetic levitation, one can reach the western city of Nagoya from central Tokyo (200 miles apart) in only about 40 minutes, while the present bullet train takes about 90 minutes – and a car, several hours – to negotiate the 200-mile distance (news.discovery.com, 2012).

Some other examples:

- Cetron and Davies in their article, "Trends shaping tomorrow's world, Part two" (May–June 2008), claim "a person's professional knowledge is becoming outdated at a much faster rate than ever before." This is caused by rapid changes in the job market and work-related technology. Do you think continuous retraining and instruction in all types of job is practical or effective? Would you suggest that anyone should just get hired straight from pre-school and do the training in the office?

- If humans can live and stay vibrant, healthy and productive in their 70s and 80s or even beyond, why haven't we changed the retirement age of 65?
- More and more companies prefer to hire young graduates who are techno-savvy and who know "more" about the world and the future; why don't we scrap longevity bonuses and instead reward the early leavers to make way for new hires?

Humorous

As the cliché goes, laughter is the best medicine. It cures boredom and lifts spirits. An appropriate joke, anecdote or irony works well to create a positive vibe among the participants. However, you should not overuse it.

Quick, ironic jokes found around the internet:

- A woman found her husband in the kitchen shaking frantically, almost in a dancing frenzy, with some kind of wire running from his waist towards the electric kettle. With quick resolve, she decided to jolt him away from the deadly current, she whacked him with a handy plank of wood, breaking his arm in two places. Up to that moment, he had been happily listening to his iPod. (Excellent for sessions in ideation and perception or interpersonal behaviours.)
- Why don't fish drown?
- "I see," said the blind man to his deaf wife as he stuck his wooden leg out the window to check if it was raining.
- Why don't they sell mouse-flavoured cat food? Who tastes dog food when it has a "new and improved" flavour?

The "punch" formula is applicable to all presentations during the facilitation process and not just at the start of the session. Use this as a guide also in framing thought-provoking questions and scenarios to enrich presentation material. It is better to combine some of the elements, as seen in the examples. Vary the style of presentation. Too much of one thing won't help. Whether you tug at their heartstrings, give them a kick in the teeth, stir their alarm bells, make them laugh or take them by surprise, the participants will tune in if their emotions are in play. Aim for that loud, pained, involuntary gasp or that silent, spontaneous, excited grin.

At the beginning of the session, the facilitator should have already addressed some nagging questions such as, "So what? What good will this give me? Will this be a waste of time?" and so on. The four quadrants of opening illustrate how this may be done. This is discussed later, in Chapter 5. By doing the four quadrants of opening, members will feel that they are being listened to at the beginning of the session.

Learning point: Slow down and double-check!

- I have facilitated many different types of events/interventions overseas in countries where English is a second or even third language.
- I have been complimented and thanked on many, many occasions about the clarity and speed of my (accent and) speaking.
- In my experience, too many even experienced facilitators forget about this or just get it wrong.
- Some seem to feel that the onus is on the group being facilitated to understand what the facilitator is saying!
- This is a very basic thing that is easily forgotten and/or underestimated.

DURING THE FACILITATION

The facilitator keeps the group path going and reaching forwards by standing out of their light or by showing them the light. When things go dark and bleak, the facilitator must be doing something wrong or, perhaps, not doing anything. When the group runs into a wall, the facilitator helps them unblock the way. This takes considerable diligence, skill and timing.

The two most crucial responsibilities of the facilitator to sustain momentum at the height of the proceedings are related to task and maintenance. Task functions aim to keep focus to purpose, sustain an efficient group process and help the team move forwards, while maintenance functions aim to maximise involvement, maintain healthy and productive social interactions and build team spirit and group identity (Hunter 2006).

During the course of the proceedings, there will always be problems and issues – which we call "blocks" – that will stand in the way, regardless of how well the session is prepared. The facilitator has to be quick to notice these problems and perform the role of the unblocker and enabler. Several facilitation problems have been mentioned or discussed in other portions of this book. In addition, here are some dilemmas that facilitators may find themselves in.

What If the Group Resists Being Facilitated?

They resist explicitly by saying they don't need a facilitator, or worse, simply don't acknowledge your presence. They may verbally attack you and question your credibility. They implicitly resist by refusing to follow prescribed processes or by disagreeing just for the sake of disagreeing, or by resorting to random discussions or deliberately veering away from the agenda.

Proposed strategy: Never ever leave the room. Don't get angry and don't let issues of self-esteem affect your disposition. Stay, but don't fight. You can facilitate surreptitiously at first, and then stealthily wedge yourself in by asking quick questions, paraphrasing, synthesising and summarising. You may also make a compromise by agreeing to handle some parts of the discussion and allowing other parts to be left to the group's control. But when the group gets out of control, you have to assert your role as a facilitator.

Point out the problem and how it has affected the group's productivity. Make them realise that they are not making any progress and they are just wasting time and energy. Suggest putting the unrelated issues in a parking lot and returning to them when the group is finished with its original agenda.

What If the Group Is Pressed for Time?

This is usually the result of failure to pace activities properly and observe time limits for discussions, which usually take the longest time.

Proposed strategy: Remind the group of the time constraints and emphasise the need to take action. Suggest to the group to prioritise which issues need to be resolved immediately and which issues may be put in the parking space to be dealt with later or in a future session. The key is to let them decide which issues are more important and urgent.

What If the Team Is Going around in Circles?

Sometimes, teams find it hard to put to a close the discussions and agree on a decision. They may be unwilling to finish brainstorming or sometimes several superfluous issues have emerged and the members unnecessarily spend time and effort discussing them.

Proposed strategy: If you think the group has gathered enough options to work on, you can suggest that they could form a decision from the ideas on the table. Summarise what has been discussed and emphasise the core points. Lead the conversation by saying, "It seems that the group has come out with a good number of suggestions. Perhaps, it's time to prioritise these options and make a decision." You could also use the time-boxing strategy: Announce that the group has X more minutes of discussion before they need to make a decision. Emphasise that the next topic on the agenda is as important. If a decision still cannot be reached, propose that the issue be put in the parking space in the meantime.

What If the Group Ignores Its Own Rules?

Sometimes, members change their minds in the middle of the session and refuse to observe the rules they have previously agreed to.

Proposed strategy: Remind them that they have agreed on what behavioural rules to follow. If you notice resistance, you may ask them what part of the rules they find difficult to follow and if they want to change the rules. However, be careful about changing rules frequently. This gives the wrong signal to the members and they will take the next set of rules as they did the first. You may also ask them how the group can ensure that members follow the ground rules.

Encourage them to police each other (peer pressure) since *they* have decided the rules by themselves. Use of a yellow and red card system may be helpful here.

Other dilemmas or behavioural problems are lack of focus, refusing to accept responsibility, scapegoating, groupthink, factions and cliques, getting stuck on only one choice, cheap closure, rambling participants, big egos and dominators.

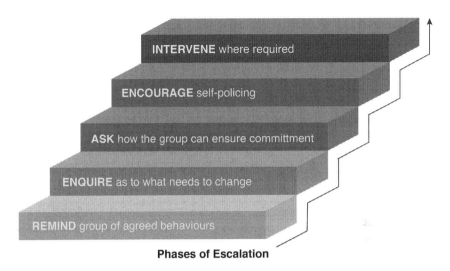

Phases of Escalation

FIGURE 2.3
Phases of escalation.

Additionally, there are also the so-called group disrupters and interrupters that are common in meetings of any kind, such as the know-it-all member, the *I don't care* member and so on. The first question the facilitator asks is, "When is intervention needed?" Sometimes, some problems are normal and need not be checked. However, there are behaviours that tend to be repetitive and escalate to a degree that disrupts group processes and, therefore, need to be addressed (Figure 2.3).

After noticing an unproductive behaviour, the facilitator determines the reason for it, plans the most appropriate action and then takes action accordingly. Sometimes all you need to do is let the group take a break. Whether there is a need to intervene is dependent on certain factors.

Below are some questions that may guide you in deciding whether intervention is warranted:

- *How serious is the problem? Might it go away by itself?*
- *Is it appropriate to intervene? What happens if I do nothing? Or, if I do nothing, will another member intervene?*
- *Do I have the time to make an intervention?*
- *Will the intervention disrupt the group process? How?*
- *Will anyone be offended?*
- *What's the chance that the intervention will work?*
- *Do I have the skills to execute the necessary intervention?*

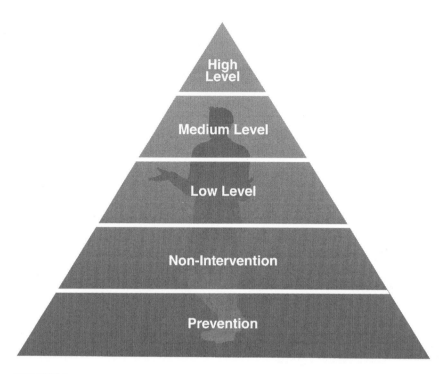

FIGURE 2.4
Levels of intervention.

The Ladder of Inference is useful in helping the facilitator understand the nature of the conflict or problem behaviour. The facilitator draws from facts, evaluates the facts and formulates decisions and courses of action based on these facts. The Ladder of Inference is presented in Chapter 3.

The degree of intervention depends upon the perceived degree of severity of a disruption. The more serious the conflict, the higher the degree of intervention.

The levels of intervention range from prevention to high-level intervention (Figure 2.4).

Prevention

An ounce of prevention is better than a pound of cure. The best way to minimise conflicts is to prevent them, but without impeding healthy debate. Here are some ways in which the facilitator could minimise conflicts in groups:

1. **Provide a clear sense of boundaries:**
   - Clarify the purpose.
   - Make individual and group expectations known.
   - Instil mutual respect.
   - Formulate and enforce ground rules.
2. **Create a sense of shared accountability and ownership:**
   - Have the group set the objectives and agree on the process.
   - Focus on the purpose and identify extraneous issues which should not be discussed.
   - Always "check in" with the group when a decision is made.
3. **Create rapport with the members and show respect for experience:**
   - Treat the members as equals but show respect for their experience.
   - Build mutual confidence among the team members and value team wisdom.
   - Engage them in conversations by having them share their experiences.
   - When you show interest in what they think, what they know and what they feel, they will tend to be more cooperative.
4. **"Buy in" power players:**
   - Identify and acknowledge the power players early on.
   - To make them feel respected, assign them some form of leadership role in activities or invite them to become your sounding boards during breaks.
   - While acknowledging the mainstream of the group, don't forget to involve the margins.
5. **Recognise important behaviours:**
   - Identify the participants with constructive behaviours and tap their potential to diffuse tense situations.
   - Take special notice of the participants who demonstrate destructive behaviours, because some conflicts will most likely be instigated by them.

     According to Brunt (1993), the following are individual behaviours that are constructive:
   - **Cooperating** – takes interest in the viewpoints of others and adapts well for group success.
   - **Clarifying** – helps in summarising, synthesising and focusing discussions.
   - **Inspiring** – helps in raising team spirit and encouraging participation and progress.

- **Harmonising** – encourages group cohesion and collaboration.
- **Risk taking** – takes risks to be embarrassed or lose opportunities for the good of the group.
- **Process checking** – helps refocus group direction by questioning and clarifying group process issues and problems.
  Brunt (1993) also identified destructive behaviours, including:
  - **Dominating** – attempts to take control of the group by use of the group's resources.
  - **Rushing** – presses the group to leave a task even before completion and dislikes listening and working with others.
  - **Withdrawing** – detaches self from discussions and activities.
  - **Discounting** – tends to flout and, to a serious degree, insult ideas and suggestions of others.
  - **Digressing** – takes away group focus by injecting unrelated issues, rambling or telling stories.
  - **Blocking** – hampers group progress by obstructing all ideas and suggestions, except their own.

6. **Most importantly, stay in your facilitator role:**
   - To remain effective, stay neutral – your biases will only serve to stir up resentments and dissatisfaction.
   - Any intervention process you introduce will most likely be rejected by the group – give objective and non-judgemental observations.
   - Don't let yourself get involved – take a step backwards, physically and mentally, and then call for a break.
   - If asked to contribute because you may be seen as an expert in a particular field, remind the group of your role and the importance of maintaining the objective boundaries.

Non-Intervention

As mentioned, there are situations when the facilitator need not intervene. Overreaction will sometimes escalate the tension. In cases where the group's momentum has been disrupted, call for a break to provide an opportunity for all heads to cool off.

Low-Level Intervention

There are several ways that the facilitator could nip tension in the bud in a non-threatening way and prevent it from escalating to a serious disruption.

After identifying the behaviour, ask yourself the probable causes of the dysfunctional behaviour. In this way, you know how to respond. You will be surprised that the tension may have actually been caused by your oversight as a facilitator. Sometimes all you need to do is to do your job well.

For example, a participant is turning the meeting into a gripe session. What you do is to reflect back or rephrase what the member said to make them feel like they're being heard. And then, after a few questions, they will be able to clarify the issue themselves.

To prevent the whole group from being unnecessarily impacted by the problem behaviour, break the group up and let them work in smaller groups. In this way, the problem behaviour will be easier to manage.

State an observation in general and address the problem as a group concern. For example: "It seems that you are now discussing an issue that falls beyond the scope of the group's purpose. How should the group address this problem?" Refer to the ground rules. Another example: "Everyone seems made up on this decision, except William and Joanne, who seem to have opposing views and who refuse to agree, either with each other or with the group. Is the group willing to accommodate William and Joanne or are you amenable to now going in the direction that most of the group wants?"

One effective way to rein in dominators is to use the wedging technique (Steve Davis, *Master Facilitator Journal*). The technique is a literal one – to *wedge* yourself in, politely and innocuously.

The process works like this: Instead of ignoring dominators, show that you are listening intently. Use body language that illustrates your focus is on them. Make the dominators feel that they are being listened to, that their opinions matter. This is because dominators tend to repeat themselves or take pride in elaborating their viewpoints unnecessarily as they are used to being ignored. Then, slowly wedge yourself in with short, verbal acknowledgements: "I see …", "Okay …", "All right …" and so on. And then, with longer statements: "What you are trying to say is …", "I feel you are telling the group that …" By taking away some of the talk time, slice by slice, you eventually end up summarising their monologues and retrieve the floor for the other members. Verify from them if your summary is accurate. Allow them to talk some more if they have anything else to add. If they resume talking and won't stop, politely ask them if you have misunderstood their ideas. Usually, this gets to them and they eventually yield.

Medium-Level Intervention

When low-level intervention fails, it's time for the facilitator to call for a break and call the attention of the errant member outside the halls of the session. Politely, but firmly, state how the disruptive behaviour is affecting the group and that the behaviour has to end, but also ask the underlying causes of their behaviour and, perhaps, assure that you will try your best to find ways to thresh out these concerns. Emphasise that working collaboratively and avoiding blocks to the group processes is for the benefit of all.

High-Level Intervention

This is necessary when disruptive behaviour is blocking the group success, harassing or causing harm on others or assailing the standing of the facilitator. It is necessary to solicit the support of the group when you give an intervention in public. Since high-level interventions are risky, they have to be worded carefully.

There are three rules to follow:

Step 1

Say what you're seeing as you see it, with no judgement and no attribution to motive or the cause of problem behaviour. Do not blame or accuse. It is based solely on observations of actual events. For example: "John, you have expressed a lot of valuable opinions, but you also refuse to listen to others. That can intimidate them into not speaking."

Step 2

Make an impact statement. Tell the member how their actions are affecting the group or the process or other people. Example: "There are still many members who would like to share their ideas, too, but cannot butt in out of respect. The group has only about an hour left and there are still many topics pending on the table."

Step 3

Redirect the person's behaviour. This can be done by 1) asking the member for their suggestions about what to do (Example: "What can you do to make sure everyone is given the chance to talk?") or 2) telling the members what to do (Example: "Please keep still for a moment, speak only when acknowledged and strictly observe the one-minute rule"). Asking is always better than telling, but when the member cannot be moved to discard their dysfunctional behaviour, *telling* will be the best thing to do.

In cases where intervention is needed, the facilitator has to do something about the situation, otherwise you will lose your credibility. Remember, the group knows what's happening and if you are honest – and if you don't attempt to cover it up – the group will support you.

Another crucial skill that a synergistic facilitator has to develop is the ability to manage conflict-habituated groups. There are conflicts that are normal and are easily handled, but there are conflicts that could spell team failure. Sometimes, the purpose of the facilitative activity is conflict resolution itself. Facilitating conflicts is one of the more complex tasks a facilitator has. Chapter 4 deals with conflicts and conflict resolution. It explains the problem-solving process, which is applicable in all types of facilitated groups.

Learning point: Don't shirk away from having to deal with a disruptive participant in a meeting/workshop.

- I was facilitating a Continuous Improvement Workshop of middle managers from the maintenance function across the UK. I was working with a co-facilitator on this workshop.
- These workshops followed a defined process and had run extremely successfully with other groups on at least ten occasions during the previous year. The results had been outstanding.
- The pre-workshop communication to the participants was clear and pitched at the right level of detail in terms of the workshop objectives and the agenda and process to be followed. They were nominated to attend by their bosses.
- There were 12 participants on this occasion.
- It became apparent early that one individual was out to be deliberately disruptive and argumentative. This was obviously being noticed by the other participants, some of whom were becoming frustrated, others embarrassed. (I later established that at the time the guy in question had a "chip on his shoulder" due to having been turned down for a promotion a few days earlier.)

- At the first break, I took the guy to one side and asked him if he had any issues with the workshop or the way we were doing things. He said that he didn't. I pointed out to him the impact that his negative behaviour and comments were having on the meeting and asked him to consider the way in which he was conducting himself. I let him know that it wasn't acceptable and we couldn't continue with him behaving in that way.
- After the break, things didn't show much of an improvement. So during a session that my co-facilitator was running, I asked "Mr Disruptive" to join me for a word outside the meeting room.
- I had already spoken with his boss, and handed him my mobile phone. His boss told him in a very straightforward way to either get a grip or get back to site and forget about attending the workshop and he would send another member of their team to attend.
- He stayed, thought better of his earlier behaviour, contributed well and apologised.

ENDING THE FACILITATION

Journeys must end even though there may be feelings of uncertainty about objectives having been met or that efforts have been enough or problems have been resolved. There is often a lack of desire for closure, a hesitation to end. It is the facilitator's responsibility to convey that something has been achieved and that the participants could work on what they have learned and that the process will continue. The facilitator initiates this sense of resolution. No matter how the journey has progressed, the facilitator should end with a powerful finish. Finish with a bang, as Reynolds suggests. The goal is to make the message loud and clear.

Create the finishing touch with whatever has been accomplished – with whatever the participants have gone through – so that, in the end, the participants will claim ownership of their achievements. The conclusion must necessarily flow from what happened, not be esoteric or abstract, so that it creates a disconnect. On this, Reynolds suggests that the message must be "sticky". The Heath brothers, Chip and Dan, who wrote the book *Made to Stick: Why Some Ideas Survive and Others Die*, lay out the critical elements of a sticky idea: Simplicity, Unexpectedness,

Concreteness, Credibility, Emotions and Stories. The facilitator may choose a combination of these elements to make the conclusion of the activity relevant, memorable and worth pursuing. The goal is to make people care, as the authors suggest.

The "Rose, Thorn and Bud" is one way to invite feedback to foster the process as it continues. It incorporates the elements of concreteness, emotions and stories. Facilitators may use a shortened rose, thorn and bud activity after a particular activity or at the end of the day.

The participants take turns telling their "rose", which signifies their favourite experience, or their "thorn", if any, which is their least favourite. Encourage them to tell their "bud", or what they look forward to or what they are committed to act on. The rose may perhaps be the most important thing they have learned; the thorn, the least relevant or least helpful of all; and the bud, a commitment to do what ought to be done.

By inviting feedback and a promise, the facilitator enhances commitment to the group's decision. This is because a participant will strive to be consistent with his or her commitment no matter how small. It is also advisable to make them write down their commitment and stick it on the board, because a written promise that is visible or made public catalyses internal conviction. The person will most likely avoid dissonance with their pledge.

One important thing that the facilitator has to do is to end the rose, thorn and bud session on a positive note. Highlight the achievements of the group and acknowledge contributions and efforts and also the necessity of further reflection and sustained commitment.

Synthesising and summarising are important components of closure. It gives a sense of resolution. The facilitator makes sure that the group has detailed action plans. Write them on the board or a flipchart. In synthesising and summarising, concentrate on the core points and discard the extraneous. This incorporates the element of simplicity.

Part of the summary should be the list of issues stored on the parking space. Have the group prioritise these issues and give general suggestions as to how these issues may be resolved.

Just after – or just before – you wind up the session, you may go back to the story in your opening. Resolve that opening, fill the gaps and provide the climax. For example, in the story of the young girl who cannot feel pain, give a short narrative of how she has learned to overcome her challenges. In relation to the Jewish girl who drew the circles as her home, tell the group about how refugees have been welcomed into the homes of strangers. That small blue dot – make it bigger and focus on what the earth has become. There are many possibilities on how to do this, but the rule is to break the disconnect and instil a sense of closure.

Another part of the closing process is evaluation. The facilitator may opt to request written or verbal evaluations or both. This sends the important message to the participants that the process is not over. Also, the evaluation offers feedback on how well facilitators have performed their functions.

Other things that the facilitator should do at the end of the facilitation process include:

- Creating an agenda for the next session.
- Having the group decide on a means for follow-up and clarifying the facilitator's role in the follow-up process.
- Providing participants with resources to encourage their continued involvement.

Keep it short. Make it count. When the participants walk out the door, they should feel that it is *their* journey now to carry forwards. And, most importantly, do not forget to say, "Thank you."

AFTER THE FACILITATION (FOLLOW-UP)

The session is over, but in some ways the work may only be starting. This is the core message of following up. Follow-up and follow-through are critical to moving (or pushing) the group's action plan. No matter how formal or informal the facilitation process has been, having a mechanism for follow-up has its benefits.

A follow-up sustains group momentum. It signals to the members that the adjournment was not the end. A follow-up conveys that work is to continue. A follow-up enables people to take stock. Follow-up activities prompt people to take stock of where they have got to. In following up, the facilitator reminds people that they are accountable for their decisions and are responsible for implementing what they have agreed to in the facilitated session. Whatever the method agreed upon, the follow-up should lay the table for evaluation of group and individual progress.

Methods of follow-up can include:

- General meeting.
- Paired groups or small groups.

- Phone interviews.
- Written progress reports.

The more promptly and consistently the meeting facilitators follow-up and follow-through on their commitments to supporting the meeting process, the greater the level of respect and attention they will command from meeting participants.

CHAPTER SUMMARY

The key points of this chapter are to understand:

- The facilitation process, and its six dimensions: Planning, meaning, confronting, feeling, structuring and valuing.
- The importance of the basics on planning and setting up the venue, how to start the facilitation and setting the mood for the session, with simple techniques to engage the participants.
- How to use humour, how to challenge, how to intervene and bring the conversation back on track during a facilitation.
- How to bring the session to a close, ensuring the participants feel they have contributed, satisfied with the outcome and any subsequent actions.
- The definition of what facilitation is and what it is not, and what should be the expected outcomes of a facilitated session.
- The role of a facilitator and situations of when to use an external facilitator and when as a leader you should facilitate.
- There are different types of facilitator for different situations and the key focus areas for each situation.
- The key principles of facilitation independent of the situation and role they need to play.

Section II

Core Facilitation Skills

3

Mastering Facilitation: Behavioural Techniques in Facilitation

Presenting naked is connecting and engaging with an audience, whether three people or 3000, in a way that is direct, honest and clear.

Teachers have been taught that the best visual aid is the teacher himself or herself. Likewise in facilitation, the best tool that the facilitator has is his or her person. As articulated in the introductory quote above, the facilitator teaches more through being than doing.

In my years of facilitating groups and in all the extensive trainings and preparations, I have learned that facilitation engages my whole being, all my senses, all my feelings and intuitions, all my energies and skills. But there are certain facilitation principles that stand out and facilitative behaviours that work along the gamut of facilitation activities.

I find that the ideas of Garr Reynolds regarding presentation capture these values and principles in the field of facilitation. The essential ingredients outlined by Garr Reynolds are germane to how a facilitator could successfully steer groups towards synergy.

I have also found that two of the most potent techniques that a facilitator could use in all facets and in all situations in the facilitation process are listening and questioning. While a variety of group processes and techniques are available for specific objectives, listening and questioning are the all-pervading skills. That is why I have concentrated on these two skills.

Listening and questioning are interrelated. An effective facilitator can frame good questions, but if he fails to listen, it will be moot. Effective listening includes skilful questioning to be able to understand everyone's perspective. Related to questioning skills are inferential skills or reasoning processes. Listening and questioning skills largely depend on how we perceive and process facts and experiences. I have included a section on the Ladder of Inference to show this.

CORE VALUES OF MASTERING FACILITATION

The keywords in Reynolds' advice are naked, connecting, engaging, direct, honest and clear. Anchored on these concepts, we could attempt to describe the values of a naked facilitator.

A naked facilitator engages with a group most effectively by being direct, honest and clear.

One of the best things to do is to "go with the flow" – you need to help the group towards a defined outcome, but also allow yourself to be flexible with your plans subject to the group's mood.

To be an effective facilitator – and, in turn, run an effective facilitation session – you should understand, embrace and demonstrate the following core values:

Flexibility

The ability to fulfil different group roles, leader, supporter, inquisitor, etc., in order to keep the group process fluid and maximise potential.

Confidence

To instil confidence in the group by appearing purposeful and in control, therefore, subduing group insecurities.

Authenticity

To be consistent in the approach to the task and not "moving the goalposts", and in doing so, becoming trustworthy to the group.

Integrity

To be an example to the group of how to conduct oneself at work. To have the admiration of the group as being a person whose judgement they can trust.

Patience/Perseverance

To appreciate the difficulties of group work and have the determination to see a task finished.

Leadership (Presence)

To have the respect of the group to become the surrogate leader if and when required.

Initiating

To be able to start the group working on the task, or when a problem is discovered/developed, to find an alternative way around it to maintain the working continuum.

Perceptive

To have the capability to recognise undertones in the group, using the positive ones to the group's advantage and countering the negative ones to diminish them.

Mastering facilitation also requires the facilitator to understand – and whenever possible, demonstrate – the importance of the following:

- Imparting of information.
- The instillation of hope (potential of resilience in adversity).
- Altruism (others offering support and reassurance).
- Universality (learning that others have similar feelings).
- Corrective recapitulation of the primary family group (family of origin work).
- Developing socialising techniques (incorporating interpersonal feedback).
- Imitative behaviour (observing modelling interactions).
- Interpersonal learning.
- Group cohesiveness.
- Catharsis (the process of expressing strong feelings that have been affecting you so that they do not upset you anymore).

Think conversations, not performance. "Just like a good conversationalist, a presenter with good presence will connect with you on some level and demonstrate with sincerity that, at least for the moment, he or she does not wish to be anywhere else than right there having a dialogue with you."

Learning point: The importance of trust, neutrality and transparency on the part of the facilitator.

- I was asked to facilitate a meeting between a company and trade unions (TU) about some big changes to working arrangements.
- The discussions were emotive and had become bogged down. I was asked to facilitate a session with a view to getting them "unstuck".
- I was introduced by the chairman of the TU side as someone the TU representatives could trust as I had always "done what I said I would do" in the past, had always kept my word and acted fairly, and had no axe to grind regarding this particular issue.
- I myself reinforced my neutrality and objectivity and at the outset I laid out my stall in terms of ground rules for the meeting, including the need for frankness and transparency in terms of discussing the real issues.
- During the course of facilitating a full day's discussion, I was able to remove the emotion from the negotiation, help the group focus on the root issues, understand each other's positions more clearly and get to the stage where they were ready to make real progress.

THE ART OF LISTENING

If you're talking, you're giving information and therefore giving away power; if you're listening and asking questions, you're gaining information, the raw material of knowledge, and therefore gaining power. Listening is part of communication. To listen is to communicate without words. It is a way of striking conversations with the group. Listening has both cognitive and emotional benefits. It promotes mutual understanding and respect in each member of the group. The esteemed Henry David Thoreau said, "The greatest compliment that was ever paid me was when one asked me what I thought, and attended to my answer." When the facilitator lends an empathetic ear, the members feel valued and there is a greater chance that the members will mirror this behaviour to you and to the others.

Active listening is a fundamental skill in facilitation. Without it, a facilitator fails – completely. Listening is a way of being open and "surrendering" to the group by removing all filters and focusing on effective and productive interactions so that synergy is achieved. Synergistic listening is the skill of the facilitator in being able to listen to both the individual and listen to the entire group at the same time. Synergistic listening is being acutely perceptive, like having aural senses in all parts of your body.

Synergistic Listening Is Deliberate

Listening is more than hearing. It requires conscious effort. It requires focus. The facilitator suspends thought processes and focuses full attention on the speaker. Listening half-heartedly, or inattentively, can be insensitive and hurtful.

Synergistic Listening Is Empathetic

To listen empathically is to seek to understand not to be understood. It requires a desire to understand. To listen is to put yourself in the speaker's shoes, to look at the world through their lenses. To be empathetic means to discard personal filters (values, assumptions, prejudices and personal experiences) that muddle deeper understanding.

Synergistic Listening Is Multisensory

It uses all senses, not just the ears. It is to listen not just to the words, but to the feelings and underlying needs: not just to the story, but to the voice. It means to listen to what is said and how it is said. And to listen also to what is unsaid or only partially said. The facilitator observes the body language of the speaker – the consistencies in verbal and non-verbal messages to get to the core of the message. It is to also feel the emotions in the message and comprehend the nuances to enhance understanding. Listening only to spoken words is inaccurate listening.

Synergistic Listening Is Active

It involves the whole body. Active listening means using body language, gestures and other forms of acknowledgement to show that the facilitator is listening. It is to respond appropriately to the speaker with verbal and non-verbal cues. Listening without showing any emotion or any form of encouragement is unproductive. However, listening should not be disruptive or interruptive.

Synergistic Listening Is a Learning Experience

This is true not just for the facilitator, but also for the group. Paying attention pays. Listening allows you to determine and understand a person's motivation, attitude and behaviour. Listening results in greater understanding and appreciation of the ideas, values and needs of the group, and then paves a smoother path to resolving problems and building consensus.

Synergistic Listening Is Non-Judgemental

The facilitator needs to be both broad-minded and open-minded. Show your willingness to open up your mind and see things from the speaker's perspective. Avoid expressions that are accusatory, critical or tactless. Your body language should also show respect and trust. Prejudices create a resistant and defensive mindset that hampers group processes and undermines synergy. It is listening to understand, not listening to respond.

Synergistic Listening Is Dynamic

You should listen not only to individual feelings and ideas but also to group behaviour and general outlook – or the lack of it. You feel the atmosphere, whether it is conducive to group productivity or it isn't. Listen for problems and issues that may be caused by individuals or that may stem from how group processes are performed.

I have emphasised the value of listening to the underlying messages shown in body language and the tone of voice. This is because spoken words partly derive their meaning from the intent or the underlying emotions and feelings of the speaker.

Sometimes, people say what they don't mean and mean what they don't say. They say "yes" when actually they mean "no". They say everything is okay when, deep down inside, they are in turmoil.

According to Mehrabian (1971), who pioneered research in non-verbal communication, one can determine the feelings and attitudes of people from their body language and paralinguistic expressions:

- 7% of a message pertaining to feelings and attitudes is in the words that are spoken.
- 38% of a message pertaining to feelings and attitudes is paralinguistic (the way that the words are said).
- 55% of a message pertaining to feelings and attitudes is in facial expressions.

The value of listening to body language is valuable in consensus building. Sometimes, despite reservations or full disagreement, people acquiesce to a decision to avoid further conflict or because they are not concerned at all. They just say "yes" when they mean "no". This is called "groupthink" which the facilitator has to watch out for when mediating conflicts.

HOW THE MASTER FACILITATOR LISTENS

There are three ways of listening: listening by attending verbally, non-verbally and para-verbally. These three aspects actually represent the three components of communication: verbal messages (spoken words), non-verbal messages (body language) and para-verbal messages (how words are uttered). These types of listening skills should be carried out simultaneously.

The facilitator shows he is in the moment through honest and active listening. You send the message that you are in the moment, right here, right now – that you are totally intent to listen, assimilate and understand; that you value the message of the speaker.

Verbal Listening: Listening with Words

Reflective listening means to respond to the speaker with words to acknowledge receipt of the message and to clarify if the message was captured accurately. Reflective listening also allows the speaker to enrich their responses.

1. **Paraphrasing** means to reword or to repeat back what the person said, as you understood it. Paraphrasing allows clarification of ideas. This is especially useful in simplifying and synthesising long and complex answers. Paraphrasing also shows that you are listening and that you are acknowledging the speaker's contribution. For example:
   - I think you are trying to say … Is that accurate?
   - What I'm hearing is …?
   - I understood that you wanted to say that …
   - You seem to feel that …
   - If I may confirm that …
     Avoid adding information to the message. Continue rephrasing until the speaker agrees that you captured the message accurately. Otherwise, if you feel that rephrasing is not working, try mirroring.

2. **Mirroring** is repeating the speaker's exact words back to them. However, use mirroring sparingly and only in situations when accuracy is the speaker's yardstick of having been heard or understood. Otherwise, use the rephrasing technique. If the facilitator has paraphrased, but the speaker seems frustrated, mirroring may work best for the particular individual. For example:
   - In your exact words, you said … Would that be correct?
   - Let me repeat what you said … Am I accurate?

3. **Questioning** – or drawing out – helps in guiding or encouraging speakers who find it difficult to express themselves or have reservations about airing their ideas. When you draw out, you tap the latent ideas of people in the group, hence boosting creativity and synergy.
   Use expressions such as, "and?", "please continue", "what do you mean by?", "that is interesting, can you say more about that?"
   Follow-up with open-ended questions that require the speaker to elaborate answers and not just respond with a yes, no or a nod. More examples will be given in the next section on questioning.

4. **Reflecting feeling** entails focusing on the feelings, and then, paraphrasing the message. For example:
   - You are anxious over the fact that …
   - It seems that your disappointment stems from …
   - You are saying that you would be more satisfied when …

5. **Summarising** at the end of a communication clarifies the intent of the speaker and focuses the attention of the other members of the

group. Inaccurate summaries result from inattention and distraction. To provide good summaries, be adept in identifying the main points of the message.

Non-Verbal Listening: Listening with Your Body

There are many ways in which a facilitator could project attentiveness to the speaker. These are some examples of how you can let them feel that you are being held by them. Your eyes, especially, show whether you are intently listening or are bored and sleepy.

Do

- Face the speaker squarely and maintain good eye contact.
- Lean gently towards the speaker.
- Maintain an appropriate distance with the speaker and avoid touching.
- Keep an open and inviting posture.
- Be still and relaxed, but not to the point of showing a lack of interest.
- Avoid gestures of exasperation.
- Use appropriate facial or head expressions – a nod, a smile, etc.

Don't

- Roll your eyes.
- Cross your arms or your legs.
- Doodle.
- Stare.
- Fidget with your hands or with any object.
- Interrupt.

Para-Verbal Listening: Listening with Your Voice

Para-verbal listening is shown in your tone, pitch and pacing of voice. It is not what you say, but how you say it. For example, the sentence, "I didn't say you were wrong," would imply different meanings and evoke varied responses depending on which word is emphasised.

More meanings can be implied when you vary the pitch of your voice. To emphasise, much of the meaning of messages is revealed in the para-verbal aspect of communication (*how* words are spoken). In the same manner that you grasp the underlying message of the speaker from their tone, you are likewise perceived by the speaker and the group members. Keeping that in mind:

- Avoid a rapid and high-pitched voice – it may be seen as anger or frustration.
- Avoid rambling – it may be regarded as confusion and unpreparedness, or even defensiveness.
- Avoid monotone – you may be perceived to be bored or uninterested.

LISTENING TO THE GROUP: GETTING THE BIG PICTURE

The intricacy of the facilitator's function lies in how they focus on both an individual's needs and the group's wellbeing at the same time. We have said that facilitators should focus their full attention on a speaker, yet they should not be oblivious to what's happening with the other participants. The group also has a body language. It also has a voice. To be an authentic synergistic listener, one must listen to behavioural patterns and group themes.

Facilitators should be very observant and acutely perceptive to be able to gauge and make sense of what's happening and what's likely to happen. It's like having aural senses attached to different areas of the body. Develop discernment to keep senses open all the time to pick up emergent situations that may promote or otherwise hinder group processes. In order to heighten listening prowess, facilitators must free themselves of extraneous ideas and feelings. Leave personal problems at home – even your biases and fears. If you feel very strongly *against* the group's decision, never let your feelings take over your focus.

Listening to the group allows you to identify click moments – those instances that enhance the process, those random ideas and actions that make agreement possible.

How does one get the "big picture"? What could help the facilitator see not only the trees, but also the forest? How does the facilitator listen to the group?

Be culturally sensitive. This is very important. Listening to the group allows the facilitator to identify not only the visible, but also the invisible diversity. This enables you to monitor interactions in a manner that respects and that builds on diversity. Respect cultural differences, group customs and rituals.

Be adaptive. Quickly evaluate the effectiveness of a technique or activity. If you think an activity is not working well and does not help the group in developing further, be flexible and make adjustments. Be prepared to modify what you have prepared. Abandon an intervention if it does not help.

Maintain focus. When you see the group slipping away from its objective, stand in the way and keep the group on track. Remind the group of *their* agreed outcomes and objectives and challenge the group to assess if their current behaviour falls on the path to achieving those goals or not. If not, challenge the group to find the best way back.

Monitor the pace of the session and the energy level. The group has a time limit to keep. Do not push if there is no need to rush. Do not delay if there's a need to finish up. Make a mental note of who is active and who is quiet and of those who *want* to talk, but don't have the courage to do so. Create the opportunity for the "idle" members to engage too.

When you notice that agreement has been met, but the group is not aware and continues to repeat itself, make a summary of the consensus and ask the members if they agree ("It seems that the group has reached a consensus and we need now to summarise ..."). Notice also when issues have been muddled. Point out the confusion and remind the group to tackle one issue at a time ("It seems that you are discussing three different issues at the same time. I suggest that we tackle issue one first ...").

Take note of information needs, whether the group lacks information or whether it has the wrong information. Set up ways to draw out more information. If there is too much unnecessary information, weed it out.

Synergistic listening is also about coordinating efforts and ideas. It is not simply gathering more and more. The facilitator should help the group in sifting through and in synthesising ideas.

When tension escalates, harmonise. Contain behavioural problems such as disrupters, interrupters and other blocks to group process (this is discussed further in Chapters 4 and 5).

Stay in your facilitator role. Be neutral and do not attempt to convince. Don't answer questions. Instead, reflect back and ask the members to answer.

Most importantly, stay awake. Be aware. Your senses won't work properly if you become distracted, tired or lose focus.

LEARNING POINT: THE NEED TO STAY FLEXIBLE.

- I had been facilitating a number of very successful change management workshops and was asked to replicate this with a team in North America.
- In advance, I went through the workshop content, process and agenda with the workshop sponsor and we agreed that everything was looking good.
- The initial stages of the workshop went really well, but as we started to get to the middle part I sensed, through "reading the room", that the energy levels were beginning to dip ever so slightly. This had never been the case on previous occasions.
- I realised that if we stuck too much/too rigidly "to the script" during the next parts of the workshop I could be in danger of losing the interest of certain members of the group.
- So I openly told them what I had been planning to do and then described what I felt might be an even better way to keep things moving forwards.
- They really appreciated my transparency and my willingness to be flexible in the interests of the group and its outcomes.
- The energy levels rocketed and we were buzzing for the remainder of the workshop.
- The participants became strong advocates for the workshop and the approach we had adopted.

THE ART OF SYNERGISTIC QUESTIONING

It's not having the right answers but asking the right questions that matters. Clichéd but, indeed, questioning is the best way to open up opportunities for learning and to keep open limitless possibilities in creating synergy.

Hence, one of the most important skills of a facilitator is the ability to ask the right questions at the right time and in the right manner. As Marilee Goldberg said, "A question can alter any circumstance." A well-crafted question captures attention, arouses curiosity, stimulates thinking and imagination, motivates action and allows creative and more meaningful learning. Discussion flourishes when questions bloom. Questions lead to more questions and produce a pool of perspectives that enriches the learning experience and enhances group synergy. By failing to ask well-crafted questions, the facilitator fails.

Asking questions serves a wide variety of purposes, but unique to a facilitator's task, questioning shifts the responsibility of knowing and of learning to the group members. In asking questions, you are able to enforce your role as a process expert and maintain your neutrality. In facilitation, it is not you, but the members, who own the problems and the solutions. Asking questions shows that you focus on the participant and that you value their power and recognise that they are in control, yet you are also able to shift responsibility to them and instil a sense of ownership over their answers and their decisions – *they* identified their problems and concerns, *they* framed their understanding, *they* gave the answers, *they* presented options, *they* formed their conclusion and *they* have to be accountable for their decisions.

Blooming Questions

Having a huge arsenal makes a powerful shooter. One of the important things that a facilitator should be mindful of is to shoot various genres of questions that stimulate different levels of thinking and creativity, from simple to complex and from less significant to the critical. Benjamin Bloom provides six cognitive levels of questions (Figure 3.1).

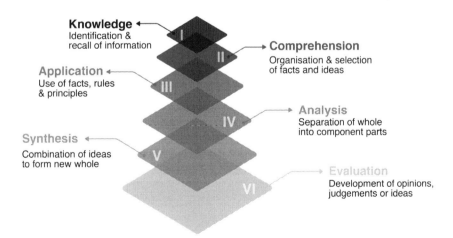

FIGURE 3.1
Bloom's taxonomy of questions.

The following are examples of questions for each level:

Knowledge Level

The learner is asked to identify or recall information without necessarily understanding the concept.

Keywords: *memorise, define, identify/name, recall, repeat, state/restate, write, list.*

Examples:

- *Can you define _____?*
- *Can you list the features of the program?*
- *Who, what, when, where, how …?*
- *What did the policy propose?*
- *What events influenced the decision?*

Comprehension Level

The learner is asked to summarise and describe, in their own words, to show understanding of a concept without relating it to other concepts.

Keywords: *describe, distinguish, explain, interpret, predict, recognise, summarise.*

Examples:

- *How do you know?*
- *Can you explain …?*
- *Can you summarise the process of …?*
- *What does it mean?*

Application Level

The learner is asked to apply facts, rules and principles to previously learned information or to their own life.

Keywords: *apply, compare, contrast, demonstrate, use, examine, relate, solve.*

Examples:

- *How does this apply to your job?*
- *Can you think of an example to fit this definition?*

- *How is ... an example of ...?*
- *How is ... related to ...?*
- *Why is ... significant?*

Analysis Level

The learner is asked to break down a whole into its component parts and describe patterns or relationships.

Keywords: *analyse, differentiate, distinguish, explain, infer, relate, separate/break down.*

Examples:

- *Can you differentiate proposition A from proposition B?*
- *What are the parts or features of ...?*
- *Classify ... according to ...*
- *Outline/diagram ...*
- *How does ... differ from ...?*
- *What evidence can you list for ...?*
- *How are these programs interrelated?*

Synthesis Level

The learner is asked to integrate different facts and ideas to form a new whole.

Keywords: *combine, create, design, develop, formulate, arrange, integrate, organise.*

Examples:

- *Can you formulate an alternative proposal?*
- *What would you predict/infer from ...?*
- *What ideas can you add to ...?*
- *How would you create/design a new ...?*
- *What might happen if you combined ...?*

Evaluation Level

The learner is asked to form opinions, judgements or decisions.

Keywords: *assess, evaluate, determine, critique, judge, justify, measure, recommend.*

Examples:

- *Can you evaluate the proposal in terms of …?*
- *Do you agree …?*
- *What do you think about …?*
- *What is the most important …?*
- *Place the following in order of priority: …*
- *Which method, procedure or solution is better?*
- *How would you decide about …?*
- *What criteria would you use to assess …?*

Bloom's categories of questions serve as a useful guide for the facilitator in preparing questions that cut across different thinking levels and learning objectives and also to diversify question types to avoid monotony.

Asking like Socrates

Asking in the Socratic tradition means allowing individuals to seek and find answers themselves through the skilful asking of a logical and coherent series of questions that extend beyond the initial answer. Subsequent questions are deduced from the initial response. It is sometimes called the "teach by asking method". Hence, this technique is most relevant to the facilitator's role of focusing on the process rather than the content. It engages more active participation in identifying implications, shaping perspectives and modifying the conditions of the original topic, issue or problem. Most importantly, doing a modern-day Socrates in facilitation is the "conversational" way of asking questions. It stimulates dialogue and a free-flowing exchange of ideas (Figure 3.2).

Noted American psychologist and expert in critical thinking R W Paul (1993) grouped Socratic questions into six categories: clarifying questions, questions that probe assumption, questions that seek for reason and evidence, questions about opinions or viewpoints, questions that probe implications and consequences and questions about the question.

Examples of Socratic questions:

1. **Questions for clarification**
   - Why do you say that?
   - Could you elaborate on that point?
   - What did you mean by the term/phrase …?

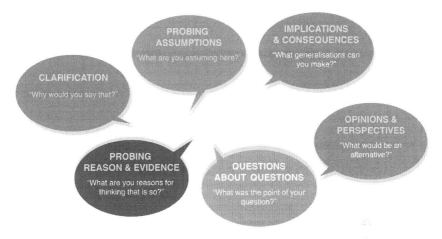

FIGURE 3.2
Types of Socratic questions (R.W. Paul).

- What's a good example of the thing you're talking about?
- How does this relate to our discussion?
- Are you saying that …?

2. **Questions that probe assumptions**
   - What are you assuming here?
   - Is this always the case?
   - Why do you think the assumption holds here?
   - What could we assume instead?
   - How can you verify or disprove that assumption?
   - Why are we neglecting C and D and including only A and B?

3. **Questions that probe reasons and evidence**
   - What are your reasons for thinking that is so?
   - What would be an example?
   - What is … analogous to?
   - What do you think caused the problem?
   - Is there good evidence for saying that?

4. **Questions about opinions and perspectives**
   - What would be an alternative?
   - What is another way to look at it?
   - Would you explain why it is necessary or beneficial, and who benefits?
   - What are your reasons for choosing … the best?
   - What are the strengths and weaknesses of …?
   - How are A and B similar?

- What is a counterargument for …?
- How would an opponent of this point of view respond?
5. **Questions that probe implications and consequences**
   - What generalisations can you make?
   - What are the consequences of that assumption?
   - When you say …, what are you implying?
   - How does … affect …?
   - How does … tie in with what you've learned before?
   - How would the results be affected by …?
   - How is that related to the issue?
6. **Questions about the question**
   - What was the point of your question?
   - What, exactly, do you mean?
   - Will you please rephrase your question?
   - Could you be more specific?
   - Why do you think I asked this question?
   - What does … mean?

Clarification goes right to the core of the Socratic tradition – dialogue (or conversation). When the facilitator seeks a clarification in the form of rephrasing, restatement or explanation, he or she extends the participation of the speaker and engages the involvement of other learners by asking them to do the restatement.

Aside from developing critical and analytical thinking, probing questions also inculcate in the learners that their ideas are acceptable, appreciated and valued. In questioning about questions, the facilitator motivates the participants to listen. It also gives them the opportunity to widen their comprehension of the question when they rephrase or justify why the question was asked or which, among their questions, are found to be the most relevant.

Socratic questions are useful in guided discussions or guided discovery techniques. A pure Socratic method does not allow the teacher to give any answer. Instead, the question may be rephrased or reframed, or another related question is asked. The modern-day facilitating Socrates also does not give answers but lays on the table relevant questions so that the participants ultimately arrive at a conclusion – or answer the original question. For example, in the Socratic decision-making process illustrated below, the original key question is how to solve a problem or issue. In the

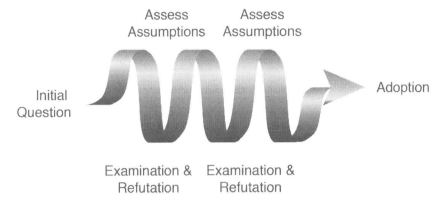

FIGURE 3.3
Illustration of Socratic method.

succeeding steps, assumptions, premises, reasoning and assessments are tested, refuted, examined and re-examined, through questions. Then, the group comes to a decision whether to adopt proposition A, proposition B, a unification of A and B or a totally different proposition. The value of the Socratic way is its potential to exhaust creative minds and energies and to offer limitless possibilities. In this way, group synergy is enhanced (Figure 3.3).

THROWING APPLES: WHAT TO ASK, WHEN TO ASK, HOW TO ASK

The framing of relevant and evocative questions is just as crucial as the timing and accuracy of delivery. Knowing what questions to ask is not enough. Giving a question, a challenge, a hint or a suggestion has to be timed to when it best serves the purpose of the group. The APPLES technique may be used as a questioning strategy.

APPLES is an acronym for:

- **A**sking the question.
- **P**ausing to allow comprehension and framing of response.
- **P**icking a participant to answer.
- **L**istening to the answer.

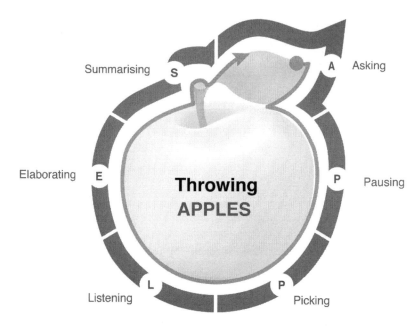

FIGURE 3.4
APPLES.

- **E**laborating on the answer.
- **S**ummarising the answer to show the general perspective (Figure 3.4).

Ask the right questions at the right time and in the right manner. Be concise, clear and focused. Repeat or rephrase the question if necessary, such as when it is a complex question. Smile and ask the question enthusiastically. Speak intelligibly and audibly. Tone of voice should be firm but friendly, not threatening or accusatory. Ask one question at a time.

Pause to give time for members to reflect on the question and to think of the answer. Be patient. Be still.

Pick the learner to answer the question. Do not allow participants to monopolise discussion. Ensure that everyone participates. Use first names.

Listen. Be still. Don't interrupt. But while the participant is talking, you may give brief responses or gestures that show you are listening:

- "Go on", "yes", "okay", "oh", "so" and "uh-huh".
- Nod, make eye contact, and smile.
- Walk towards the person talking.

Elaborate on the answer. Clarify vague or confusing answers. Confirm with the participant. Otherwise, ask the speaker to explain again.

Summarise and search for consensus. Emphasise key points of the answer. Write them on the board or a flipchart for everyone to see. Synthesise the points from all respondents. Confirm with the group. Encourage feedback. *Repeat this process if you feel there is a need to ask follow-up questions.*

Below are other question types that are relevant to the facilitator's role as a process manager:

Affective Questions

Used to elicit expressions of attitude, values or feelings.
For example:

- *How do you feel about …?*
- *Is that important to you?*
- *Would you like to …?*
- *Which of the options best appeal to your sense of values?*

Managerial and Structuring Questions

Used to keep group process in momentum or to manage the setting.
For example:

- *Are there any questions?*
- *Any further comments? Any suggestions?*
- *Is the next activity clear?*
- *Are we ready to continue? Do you think we should proceed to the next step?*
- *Is there anything that needs to be done?*
- *Is this applicable/relevant to your objectives?*

Rhetorical Questions

Used to emphasise or reinforce a point.
For example:

- *Could you rephrase your answer?*
- *Would you repeat that?*
- *What's the most important lesson of the story?*

Focusing/Refocusing Questions

Used to focus/redirect group effort on a particular point.
  For example:

- *If this is true, what are the implications for ...?*
- *How does Billy's answer relate to ...?*
- *Can we analyse that answer now?*
- *We must ask the question, what then (or what if) ...?*
- *How can this framework help us understand what's happening?*

Open and Closed Questions

An open question is designed to allow the person to be totally open and free to provide any answer they have to the question. It doesn't matter if the response is one or two words or many words. The key is the question allows the person to be open and give their own response. The response quantity of words is not the point or the function, it is the intent of the question and the way our language is structured. The open question structure words will be *what, how, why, who, when, where, which, tell me, explain, describe* and so on.

The function of a closed question is to clarify, confirm or provide a choice of alternatives. The words we use to construct closed questions are *do, is, can, will, have, are, does, would-could-should* – these are all auxiliary verbs. Their function is to create a form of closure or narrowing which is the opposite of opening and is a very necessary function in high-quality conversation and facilitation.

A conversation/facilitation structure will fundamentally follow – open, open closed or open-open-open closed.

Frame a variety of questions to suit learning styles and to tap critical thinking and creativity. Use these techniques to elicit more ideas, exhaust possibilities and promote discussion. Ask open-ended questions rather than closed questions. Open or divergent questions elicit more ideas while closed questions elicit mere recall (what, where, who, when) or simple answers like "yes" or "no".

Two examples of "close-ended" questions versus "open-ended" questions:

- **Closed-ended**: *What is the definition of ...?*
- **Open-ended**: *After citing the definition of ..., can you explain the main points of the concept?*

- **Open-ended**: *What happened?*
- **Closed-ended**: *Can you narrate the details of the event and explain how the experience affected you?*

There are *some* open-ended questions that begin with *what* and *who*, and nevertheless, invite people to participate. For example:

- *In what particular instances would this be most applicable?*
- *Who else has anything to say?*
- *Who has questions about ...?*
- *What are some examples of ...?*
- *What are other alternatives that we can consider?*

Don't put people on the spot. Be sensitive to feelings and reservations. Ask third-party questions instead of direct questions. A direct question is asked simply and directly to a member, while third-party questions are framed in such a way that the members are able to express their personal thoughts, and other sensitive information, through projection. Third-party questions have two parts – the quotation/introduction and the main question seeking the individual's opinion or judgement.

Some examples of "direct" questions versus "third-party" questions:

- **Direct question**: *What do you think about the new regulatory policy of the local council?*
- **Third-party question**: *In response to the new regulations, the president of the chamber of commerce said ... What are your thoughts about his comment?*
- **Direct question**: *Do you agree with HR's decision to ...?*
- **Third-party question**: *On the recent HR decision, some people feel that ... How does that sound to you?*
- **Direct question**: *Do you find the ... relevant in your work?*
- **Third-party question**: *There is some concern about the relevance of the ..., can you relate to that concern?*

Introducing the main question with an existing and already expressed position or opinion is an indirect manner and non-threatening way of extracting ideas and feelings. The participant becomes more comfortable in answering because their answer is merely a projection of the opinion of others.

QUICK TIPS IN QUESTIONING

Below are some quick tips to remember when engaging with participants and, particularly, when asking questions:

- When in doubt, check it out – don't let vague, but relevant, issues pass.
- Use first names in addressing participants.
- Acknowledge contributions. Give praise.
- Stimulate interest by incorporating emotive phrases like:
  - *Your point is interesting ... tell us more.*
  - *I wonder why ...*
  - *That gives a unique twist to the issue ...*
  - *I think the group would like to understand how you arrived at that ...*
  - *I'm intrigued ...*
- Don't refute ideas. Throw back the issue to the members, for example:
  - Is there anyone who would give another opinion?
  - Do you think the answer adequately addresses the problem?
- Don't answer questions. Ask other participants to answer.
- Don't put people on the spot.
- Minimise "why" questions. Asking why puts the participants in a defensive stance and limits contribution. Instead of asking, "Why do you think so?" you can ask, "Could you cite evidences that support your argument?" or "Can you explain the process of formulating that conclusion?"
- Manage monopolisers and disrupters.
- While discussion is good, avoid longwinded discussions and keep watch of the time. Know when to end discussions. Use a parking space for unfinished issues or extraneous questions that are otherwise significant.
- Most importantly, prepare, prepare, prepare.

The type of questions we ask and how often we ask the right questions (habit of questioning) help us in making sound judgements on absolutely everything that happens during facilitation. As the eminent Peter Drucker said in his book *Men, Ideas and Politics*, "The most serious mistakes are not being made as a result of wrong answers. The truly dangerous thing is asking the wrong questions." When we ask the wrong questions, we get the wrong answers. Truly, there really are no wrong answers, just wrong questions.

Asking the right questions develops a rigid inferential or abstraction process. In making inferences, the facilitator subconsciously goes through stages – subconsciously, because experiencing and ideating are done almost simultaneously. If we could master this inferential process, we could develop our questioning skills and, subsequently, our knowledge and understanding of the world. The process of forming beliefs and decisions is best explained by the Ladder of Inference.

THE LADDER OF INFERENCE: A FRAMEWORK FOR MAKING MINDS MEET

There is a joke about people making assumptions. "When you assume, you make an ass of 'u' and 'me.'" How many times do we find ourselves making assumptions and then, realising later on, that we are totally wrong? And sometimes, the realisation comes a little too late. How many times have we been accused of "putting two and two together and making five" – jumping to conclusions way too fast? Conflicts usually stem from unnecessary misunderstandings. Misunderstandings occur when assumptions becloud judgement or when we are too quick to form our own conclusions.

So, to understand requires us to avoid making assumptions. The only assumption we are to make is to assume that we have misunderstood.

We make the wrong assumptions and form flawed conclusions when we fail to distinguish between the inferences we make about the experience and the experience itself. We usually draw conclusions from first impressions, without much thinking or reasoning. The stages of thinking (that is, from observation to decision to action) could be explained by the "Ladder of Inference" – a model developed by psychologist Chris Argyris, professor at Harvard and used by Peter Senge in *The Fifth Discipline: The Art and Practice of the Learning Organization*. Argyris suggests that, because we process and create inferences about our experience at lightning speed, we don't realise that we are actually experiencing and assessing the experience at the same time.

The Ladder of Inference describes the stages of how conclusions are derived from facts. From a pool of facts and realities, we select data, then interpret the data, then make assumptions, then draw conclusions, then shape our beliefs and then act, based on those beliefs (Senge et al., 1994). Each rung of the ladder indicates a filtering stage, each filter composed of our biological, social and cultural experiences (Figure 3.5).

Starting at the bottom of the ladder is *a pool of reality and facts*. From this infinite pool, we go up to the next rung, the observation rung, where we select data that strike us as relevant or significant. After selecting the facts, we go up to the next step, the explanation rung, where we interpret the selected facts by adding meaning and explaining the significance of the facts or by organising our observations and interpreting them as stories. From these interpreted realities, we go up to the next stage, the assumption rung, where we fill in the gaps in our stories with assumptions. Next is the decision rung, where we apply our assumptions to form conclusions and decide how to respond. Further up is the reinforcement rung, where our conclusions become ingrained in our belief system and further strengthen or sustain our beliefs. Finally, we reach the top of the ladder, the action rung, where we take action that seems right, because it is based on what we believe.

FIGURE 3.5
The Ladder of Inference.

Through our lives, we traverse this ladder of abstraction day in and day out and build an intricate ladder-upon-ladder of assumptions and beliefs which form our mental models, the way we unwittingly react to everything we experience. And because of the differences in experiences, different people look at the same reality in diametrically opposed perspectives and decide on these perspectives in different ways. Imagine the endless loop of ladders in a team, the chaos in all these clashing mental models. No wonder conflict in groups is inevitable.

Facilitators could use the Ladder of Inference in many ways. Most importantly:

- To develop thinking habits and overcome skilled incompetence.
- To effectively listen to individuals in the facilitated group.
- To guide a step-by-step process of making minds meet.

Chris Argyris argues that our mental models define the way we interact with others. All those bits and pieces, all those odds and ends that make up our mental models work behind the scenes in controlling how we act and react and do things. The nuts and bolts forming our beliefs determine how we engage with what we see, whether we ignore or distort the bare facts or we grasp reality as it is. And because forming beliefs is instinctive, we unwittingly lend ourselves to being incompetent in dealing with incongruities or with beliefs that deviate from ours, making us frustrated, annoyed or angry.

Chris Argyris calls this "skilled incompetence". To overcome this, we must learn to consciously work on our thinking habits.

Below are some lessons from the Ladder of Inference which we could use to overcome skilled incompetence and instil objectivity in facilitation practice.

Lesson 1: Rule Your Mind or It Will Rule You

Develop the habit of questioning your assumptions, conclusions, decisions and beliefs. Do not assume that you are always correct. Be humble and be open-minded. Before taking any action, pause and ask these questions:

- *Am I making the right conclusion?*
- *Am I assuming correctly?*
- *Is this really the right thing to do?*

- *Have I considered all the facts?*
- *How did I form this belief?*
- *Why does my opinion differ from others?*

Lesson 2: Stay as Low as You Can

Develop the habit of challenging and evaluating your thinking process. Cast doubts on your reasoning prowess. Investigate the roots of your thinking. Using the Ladder of Inference, determine what rung you are stepping on and, from your current position, retrace your steps. Work back down the ladder to evaluate your reasoning. As you do this, you may realise you have missed some facts or that you need to adjust your assumptions or that you have made the wrong conclusion altogether. The rule is that, in assessing your decision, go as low as you can.

Lesson 3: Learn to Swim before You Dive

Avoid the habit of jumping to conclusions. As you evaluate your reasoning process using the Ladder of Inference, look out for steps that you tend to miss. Are you selective in choosing data? Do you tend to make assumptions too easily? Do you tend to jump to conclusions? When you know your thinking tendencies and, therefore, your reasoning flaws, you can work on them, consciously.

Lesson 4: When in Doubt, Check It Out

Do naked reasoning. By naked reasoning, I mean getting another person to listen to your reasoning, your arguments or your plan of action and then invite feedback. Through this, you could enrich the facts and realities and scale the Ladder of Inference again.

Lesson 5: Avoid Simplification

Develop the habit of explaining and rid yourself of the "do as I say" attitude. Do not simply express your idea and impose. Develop the habit of backing up your arguments with facts.

Lesson 6: Different Folks, Different Strokes

Other people have their own mental models. Invite them, albeit innocuously, to use the Ladder of Inference in making decisions. In this way, you enhance the chance of all of you looking at the same set of facts objectively and reaching a mutually beneficial decision.

This leads us appropriately to how the facilitator can utilise the Ladder of Inference in groups. A facilitator will invariably be challenged to act on problem behaviours in groups. The Ladder of Inference guides the facilitator in objectively evaluating perceived behaviour and helps them make better intervention outcomes. Through the steps, the facilitator asks questions before going up.

At times when an intervention is not working, a quick reference to the Ladder of Inference may help the facilitator find a better way. The Ladder of Inference serves to widen the facilitator's field of judgement. As Anais Nin said, "We don't see things as they are, we see things as we are." When we have a better grasp of how we think, we have a better grasp of how others do.

The Ladder of Inference is also very useful in facilitating conflict resolution. How this may be done is explained in the chapter on group conflicts (Chapter 4).

Suffice to say, at this point, that what gets through our senses – how we view the world around us – depends on how well we question our thoughts and decisions as we encounter experiences every day (Figure 3.6).

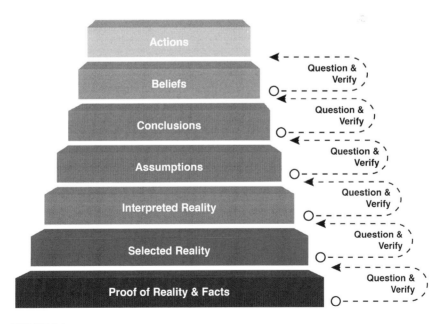

FIGURE 3.6
Applying the Ladder of Inference in facilitation.

CHAPTER SUMMARY

The key points of this chapter are to understand:

- The need to focus on the behavioural techniques in facilitation.
- The core values of mastering facilitation.
- The art of listening and how the master facilitator listens.
- The power of verbal listening techniques such as paraphrasing, mirroring, questioning, reflecting feeling and summarising.
- The non-verbal listening with your body.
- The key principles of facilitation independent of the situation and role they need to play.

4

Conflict Resolution and Decision-Making

When people have different levels of perspective, they will not see eye to eye. When people perceive things or respond to events in different ways, their interpretations often clash. When people have varying abilities, interests or inclinations, their decisions are incompatible. In short, conflict arises. When there is conflict, group process is affected.

THE NATURE OF GROUP CONFLICT

Conflict is normal in groups. Often, conflict can be beneficial. Conflict has the potential to enrich information, broaden perspectives and allow for better decision-making and outcomes. But unresolved conflict is definitely a negative thing. In group work, conflict arises from real or perceived problems regarding data, relationships, interests and values. It is imperative for a facilitator to determine the potential source of conflict between group members to be able to quickly remedy the situation (Figure 4.1).

Conflicts arising from data sources may be due to many things – the absence or the lack of information, wrong information and disregard of information or contradictory interpretations. Conflict shows up in relationships because of alliances or affiliations, miscommunication, stereotypes, repetitive negative behaviours and wrong perceptions. Conflicts relating to interests may be in the form of incompatible goals between individuals or between the individual and the organisation or competition. People have conflicting values because they have different life experiences, so their views of what is right or wrong are also

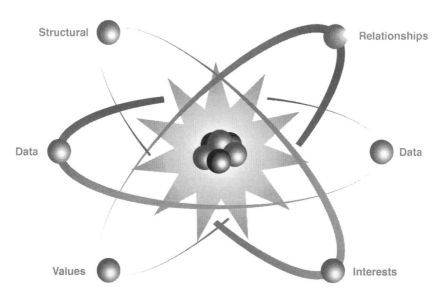

FIGURE 4.1
Potential sources of conflict.

polarised. Structural conflicts may be due to a lack of resources or power incongruence.

Conflict is defined as a phenomenon occurring between interdependent parties as they experience negative emotional reactions to perceived disagreements and interference with the attainment of their goals (Barki & Hartwick, 2001). From this definition, we can derive two dimensions of conflict – focus and manner (Barki & Hartwick, 2004). Focus of conflict pertains to task content, processes and relationships. Manner is how it occurs and whether it is cognitive, behavioural or affective (Figure 4.2).

Task conflict pertains to conflict on task content, such as conflicting goals. Process conflict is conflict about how tasks are to be carried out. Relationship conflict arises from personality differences or emotionally charged interactions due to issues of a personal nature. Disagreement is the cognitive component of conflict which occurs when there are contradictory judgements due to divergent beliefs, interests, values and goals. Interference is the behavioural component which is frequently seen in disruptive behaviour or hostility. Disagreement alone does not constitute conflict. Conflict arises only when behavioural or emotional responses interfere with the interests of another or undermine the goals of the other side. For example, debate is healthy, but when accompanied by aggression, ill will, anger or hostility, it becomes a conflict.

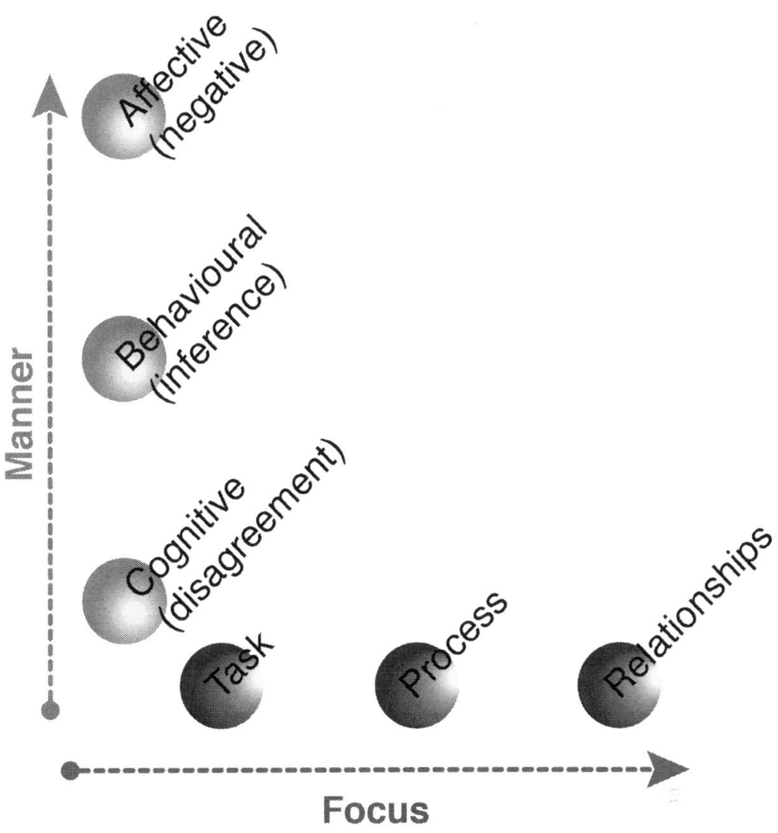

FIGURE 4.2
Dimensions of conflict.

It is important that the facilitator is able to diffuse conflicts before tension escalates. When conflict aggravates, issues may change or may spawn other issues. This brings more disputants into the picture and further complicates the facilitator's dilemma.

CONFLICT RESOLUTION

Besides, conflict resolution is rarely about honesty or establishing truth – it is more about unifying perceptions (Bodine, Crawford & Schrumpf, 1996).

"Win–win" means that agreements or solutions are mutually beneficial and mutually satisfying. With a win–win solution, all parties feel good about the decision and feel committed to the action plan.

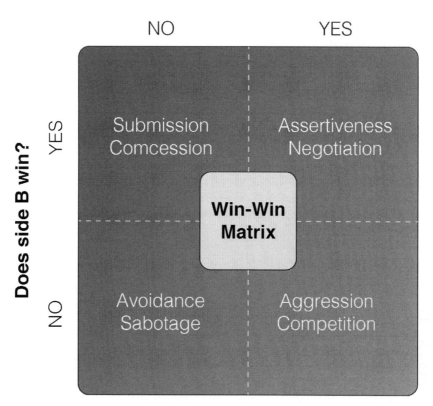

FIGURE 4.3
Win–win matrix.

The two styles of avoidance and competition are opposing conflict styles.

Avoidance is characterised by denial and hiding from the conflict, while competition is characterised by the use of power or violence to change the status quo or achieve a win–lose situation. The other styles are less severe and emphasise a willingness to work with the other party to achieve a solution. The style of collaboration is placed at the top right corner of Figure 4.3 as it is highly, but equally, concerned about the concern for the other party as well as the concern for the self. If this type of conflict style is practised by the involved parties, the conflict is most likely to be resolved as a win–win situation. Neither party would have received everything they wanted, but they both would have achieved a satisfactory portion of their goals.

Strategic Responses to Conflict

Competing Strategy

Individuals tend to pursue their own concerns at the other person's expense. They may be power-oriented and use whatever power seems appropriate to win their own position. Competitors may stand up for their rights, defend positions they believe are correct or simply try to win.

Competing strategies are best used in situations that require an unpopular decision to be made, in emergencies or when the other person is being competitive.

However, if this style is too predominant, others may be afraid to disagree or may withhold vital information from the Competitor.

If this style is underutilised, the individual may appear powerless and lacking confidence or knowledge.

Collaborating Strategy

Individuals tend to work with others to find solutions that fully satisfy the concerns of both sides. Collaborators seek to understand underlying concerns and find alternatives that meet those concerns.

Best used in situations that require innovative solutions, commitment by others or strong interpersonal relationships. If this style is too predominant, time may be spent needlessly discussing issues that don't warrant extensive attention. If this style is underutilised, opportunities for joint gain are missed, and others may not be supportive of decisions or actions.

COMPROMISING STRATEGY

Individuals tend to find some expedient, mutually acceptable solution that partially satisfies both parties. Compromising gives up more than competing, but less than accommodating.

Compromisers may split the difference, exchange concessions or seek a quick middle-ground position.

Best used to arrive at quick or temporary solutions under time pressure, when goals are only moderately important or when two opponents are strongly committed to mutually exclusive goals.

This style is useful as a backup mode when collaboration or competition fails to succeed.

Avoiding Strategy

Individuals tend to not address conflict. Rather, they diplomatically sidestep an issue, postpone dealing with conflict or simply withdraw from a threatening situation.

Best used in situations that require a cooling down period to reduce tensions. In addition, avoiding is effective when the potential damage of confronting a conflict outweighs the benefits of its resolution or when gathering more information outweighs the advantages of an immediate decision. If this style is too predominant, others may stop seeking the Avoider's input, decisions may be made by default rather than reason and inordinately high amounts of energy may be devoted to skirting issues. If this style is underutilised, the individual may devote too much time to unimportant issues or be perceived as needlessly stirring up issues.

Accommodating Strategy

Individuals tend to neglect their own concerns to satisfy the concerns of others. Accommodators may be selfless and generous. They may obey or yield to another person's point of view when they really don't want to.

Best used in situations that require the individual to build up social credits for later issues when the decision is more important to the other person or when the individual is outmatched and losing. If this style is too predominant, others may not give attention to the Accommodator's ideas and concerns. If this style is underutilised, the individual may appear unreasonable, never willing to give in.

Given the above, here are some facilitation guidelines that can be helpful when negotiating. These guidelines can be introduced formally (e.g. written up) or informally (spoken about) depending on the group's needs but will create a basis upon which negotiation takes place.

Guidelines for Negotiation

Benefits of Interest-Based Negotiation

- An outcome that meets underlying interests – the things we need or care about.
- The best of all possible ways to deal with differing interests.
- An outcome that is better than any alternative away from the table.

- A fair outcome as judged by legitimate standards.
- An outcome that strengthens the relationship.
- Discovery of issues not initially apparent that may turn out to be decisive in reaching agreement or consensus.
- Better communication resulting from improved understanding of each person's motivations.
- More creative solutions to problems.
- A durable outcome.

The negotiation method:

1. One person will present his or her view of the situation.
2. The other person will not speak except to ask clarifying questions.
3. The listener must make notes about the other person's views.
4. When the first person is finished, the second person will give a summary of what he or she heard.
5. If the first person is satisfied that he or she was heard correctly, the process will be repeated.
6. At no point will anyone interrupt, interject or argue.
7. Everyone will maintain neutral body language.
8. The facilitator can and will stop proceedings if any rule is broken.
9. Once both parties agree that they have been heard, there will be a recess, during which time each party answers two questions:
   - What I need from you to put this behind us.
   - What I'm offering you in return.
10. The parties reconvene to share their needs and offers and make a commitment to act on them.
11. All conversations will be kept confidential and not be shared with other group members.

Create Safety

Before parties speak, engage them in a conversation to set some guidelines for the conversation. Engage them in a conversation to create norms that will ensure the conversation will be comfortable. Ask them to list the rules that make it possible for them to listen respectfully and with an open mind. Ratify the new norms with both parties and record them on a flipchart. Post the new norms within clear sight of both participants.

Facilitative Listening

Randomly choose one person to present his or her views about the conflict situation or the relationship while the other person listens actively and makes notes. Strictly enforce the rules and make sure that all participants are displaying neutral body language and are asking only clarifying questions. Stop any rebuttals or arguments immediately.

Feedback

Once the first person indicates that he or she has fully shared his or her view of the situation, ask the second person to paraphrase the points made by the first person. Reinforce the need to be neutral and calm when he or she paraphrases. At the end of the paraphrasing, ask the first speaker if the other party has given a correct summary of the first party's points. If the first party feels satisfied, reverse roles and repeat the process with the second party.

Reflection

Congratulate the parties for their willingness to hear the other person. Send the parties home to reflect on what they have heard. Tell them they must not call anyone else to share confidential information. Ask them to review their notes and reflect on what they need from the other person in order to restore effective working relationships.

Attributes of Skilled Negotiators

Becoming a skilled negotiator takes patience and experience. However, most skilled negotiators share certain, common attributes that "set them apart from the pack". They:

- Resist using "irritating" words or phrases that have little persuasive value. These phrases tend to be self-praising and serve to implicate the other party negatively. For example, the skilled negotiator would not refer to his or her proposal as generous.
- Rarely respond to a proposal with a counterproposal. Immediately offering a counterproposal can complicate the negotiation. It is interjected at a moment when the other party is least receptive, and it

is often perceived by the other party as an effort to block any forward movement of the negotiation.

- Ignore statements by the other party that could be perceived as attacking and refrain from making statements of a defensive nature. They do not engage in a tit-for-tat dialogue.
- Give advance indication of what they are about to say. For example, before asking a question, they might say, "Can I ask you a question …?" Or, before making a proposal, "If I could make a suggestion …" This behaviour draws the attention of the listener and leads to clearer communication.
- Offer their reasons for disagreeing with a proposal or comment before articulating their disagreement. The less skilled negotiator would say, "I disagree with that because of …" rather than, "Let me tell you what my thoughts are on this topic, before I share my reaction to your proposal."
- Use summarising and restating techniques to reduce the likelihood of misunderstandings or misconceptions. While the less skilled negotiator may wish to promote ambiguity for fear that clarity will lead to disagreement, the skilled negotiator has a greater concern with reaching a well thought out agreement that is destined to be implemented successfully.
- Ask significantly more questions than less skilled negotiators. Provide information about their internal thought processes and feelings. For example, rather than be silent, a skilled negotiator who is doubtful about the truthfulness of a statement by the other party might say, "I'm not sure how to react to that. If what you say is true, then I would like to accept it; yet I feel some doubts about the accuracy of the information. Can you help me with this?"
- Put forth the single strongest rationale for their proposal, rather than dilute their argument by advancing multiple supporting reasons. Offering several relatively minor arguments gives the other party the opportunity to focus on the weakest link and diminishes the strongest link.

Consensus Decision-Making

Consensus decision-making is a creative and dynamic way of reaching agreement between all members of a group. Instead of simply voting for an item and having the majority of the group getting their way, a consensus group is committed to finding solutions that everyone actively supports or, at least, can live with. This makes sure that all opinions, ideas and concerns are taken into account. By listening closely to each other, the group aims to come up with proposals that work for everyone.

Consensus is neither compromise nor unanimity. It aims to go further by weaving together everyone's best ideas and most important concerns; a process that often results in surprising and creative solutions, inspiring both the individual and the group as a whole.

The following are the key elements in effective consensus decision-making.

Conditions for Consensus

As a first point, everyone in the group needs to identify and share a clear, *common goal* and be willing to work together towards it. Work out together what your goals are and how you will get there. If differences arise later, revisit the common goal to help to focus and unite the group.

Working Together

At the heart of consensus is a respectful dialogue between equals. It's about everyone working together to meet both the individual's and the group's needs – working with each other, rather than for, or against, each other, something that requires openness and trust.

Consensus is looking for win–win solutions that are acceptable to all. No decision will be made against the will of an individual or a minority. Instead, the group adapts to all its members' needs. If everyone agrees to a decision, they will all be much more committed to making it happen.

Consensus decision-making is based on the idea that people should have full control over their lives and that power should be shared by all, not just concentrated in the hands of a few. It's about having the freedom to decide one's own course in life and the right to play an equal role in creating a common future. This is why it is used widely in groups working towards a more just and equitable society, such as small voluntary groups, co-operatives and campaign networks.

Commitment to Reaching Consensus

Everyone needs to be willing to really give it a go. This means being deeply honest about what it is you want or don't want, and properly listening to what others have to say. Everyone must be willing to shift their positions, to be open to alternative solutions and be able to reassess their needs.

Trust and Openness

Everyone needs to be able to trust that everyone else shares their commitment to consensus and respects all opinions and rights equally. It would be a big breach of trust for people to manipulate the process of the meeting in order to get the decision they (the individual) most want.

Part of this process is to openly express both desires (what we'd like to see happening) and needs (what we have to see happen in order to be able to support a decision). If everyone is able to talk openly, then the group will have the information it requires to take everyone's positions into account and to come up with a solution that everyone can support.

Sufficient Time

Sufficient time is essential for making decisions and for learning to work by consensus. Taking time to make a good decision now can save wasting time revisiting a bad one later.

Clear Process

It is essential to have a clear process for making decisions and to make sure that everyone has a shared understanding of how it works.

Active participation: in consensus, we all need to actively participate. We need to listen to what everyone has to say, voice our thoughts and feelings about the matter and proactively look for solutions that include everyone.

Facilitation

In most meetings, there are one or more facilitators. Their role is to ensure that the tasks of the meeting get done and that decisions are made and implemented. They also help the group to work harmoniously, creatively and democratically.

The facilitators might take steps to keep the meeting focused or make sure a few people don't dominate the discussion. They might suggest a break when people are getting tired. They might have prepared an agenda and process that will help the group achieve its goals.

The facilitators shouldn't have any more power than anyone else and should stay neutral on the issues under discussion. They're not there to make all the proposals and decide things for a group. They can only do their job with everyone's support and co-operation.

If a small group doesn't give anyone the role of a facilitator, then everyone can be responsible for making the process of the meeting work.

Key Skills for Consensus

Active Listening

When we actively listen, we suspend our own thought processes and give the speaker our full attention. We make a deliberate effort to understand someone's position and their needs, concerns and emotions.

Summarising

A succinct and accurate summary of what's been said so far can really help a group move towards a decision. Outline the emerging common ground as well as the unresolved differences: "It seems like we've almost reached agreement on that bit of the proposal, but we need to explore this part further to address everyone's concerns." Check with everyone that you've got it right.

Synthesis

Find the common ground and any connections between seemingly competing ideas and weave them together to form proposals. Focus on solutions that address the fundamental needs and key concerns that people within the group have.

A Consensus Flowchart

There are many different ways of reaching consensus. This model outlines the common stages and will work well with up to about 20 people.

The Decision-Making Process

Figure 4.4 shows how a discussion evolves during the consensus process. At the beginning, it widens out as people bring different perspectives and ideas to the group.

This provides the material needed for a broad-ranging discussion which explores all the options and helps people understand each other's concerns.

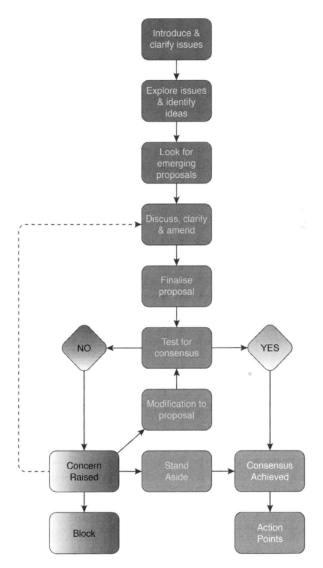

FIGURE 4.4
Consensus flowchart.

This can be a turbulent and sometimes difficult stage – people might be grappling with lots of competing or contradictory ideas – but it is the most creative part, so don't lose heart!

Then, the group moves on to synthesise a proposal (Figure 4.5). This means finding the group's common ground, weeding out some ideas and combining all the useful bits into one proposal. Finally, if the group agrees on a proposal, a decision is reached and implemented.

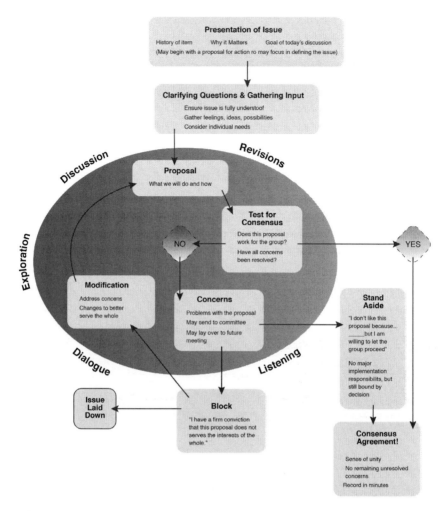

FIGURE 4.5
Developing consensus.

Guidelines for Reaching Consensus

Below are guidelines that will assist you in – and are important to demonstrate your command of – any negotiation:

- If you don't understand something, don't be afraid to say so.
- Be willing to work towards the solution that's best for everyone, not just what's best for you. Be flexible and willing to give something up to reach an agreement.
- Help to create a respectful and trusting atmosphere. Nobody should be afraid to express their ideas and opinions. Remember that we all

have different values, backgrounds and behaviour and we get upset by different things.

- Explain your own position clearly. Be open and honest about the reasons for your viewpoints. Express your concerns early on in the process so that they can be taken into account in any proposals.
- Listen actively to what people are trying to say. Make an effort to understand someone's position and their underlying needs, concerns and emotions. Give everyone space to finish and take time to consider their point of view.
- Think before you speak, listen before you object. Listen to other members' reactions and consider them carefully before pressing your point. Self-restraint is essential in consensus – sometimes the biggest obstacle to progress is an individual's attachment to one idea. If another proposal is good, don't complicate matters by opposing it just because it isn't your favourite idea! Ask yourself: "Does this idea work for the group, even if I don't like it the best?" or "Does it matter which one we choose?"
- Don't be afraid of disagreement. Consensus isn't about us all thinking the same thing. Differences of opinion are natural and to be expected.
- Disagreements can help a group's decision, because with a wide range of information and opinions, there is a greater chance the group will find good solutions. Easily reached consensus may cover up the fact that some people don't feel safe or confident enough to express their disagreements.

Agreement and Disagreement

At the decision stage people have several options:

Agreement with the Proposal
You are willing to let the project go ahead, in its current form.

Reservations
You are willing to let the proposal go ahead but want to make the group aware you aren't happy with it. You may even put energy into implementing it once your concerns have been acknowledged.

Standing Aside
You want to object but not block the proposal. This means you won't help to implement the decision, but you are willing for the group to go ahead

with it. You might stand aside because you disagree with the proposal, or you might like the decision, but be unable to support it because you don't have the time or energy.

The group may be happy to accept the stand aside and go ahead, or they may work on a new proposal, especially if there are several stand asides.

Blocking

A block always stops a proposal from going ahead. It expresses a fundamental objection. It isn't "I don't really like it" or "I liked the other idea better". It means that you cannot live with the proposal. The group can either start work on a new proposal or look for amendments to overcome the objection.

In an ideal consensus, processing a block wouldn't happen since any major concerns about a proposal should be addressed before the decision stage. However, sometimes people aren't able to express their concerns clearly enough or aren't heard by the group. In such situations, the block acts as a safeguard to ensure that decisions are supported by everyone.

Being able to block is an integral part of consensus, but it comes with a big responsibility. A block stops other people from doing something that they would like to do, and it should therefore only be used if serious concerns are unresolved.

Make sure everyone understands the different options for expressing disagreement. Often people are confused and block when they'd actually be happy to stand aside. Sometimes people are scared of blocking, even if they are deeply unhappy and use a milder form of disagreement instead.

Consensus in Large Groups

In large groups, it's a good idea to delegate issues to smaller groups, such as working groups or local groups. However, sometimes the issues will be so important that they have to be discussed and decided by everyone. This will often be done in a *spokes council*, which enables hundreds and thousands of people to work together, by consensus, in an efficient way.

In a spokes council, the meeting splits into small groups, which start by discussing the issue(s) to come up with concerns and ideas. Spokes (delegates) from each group then meet up in a spokes council to relay these thoughts.

The spokes council uses this information to create one or more proposals. These are discussed back in the small groups to check for any amendments and agreement. The results of these discussions are taken to the spokes council who should be able to either confirm agreement or draw up new proposals for further discussion. In this way, the power to make decisions lies firmly with the small groups, not the spokes.

The small groups are often based around pre-existing groups such as work teams, local groups or affinity groups. Alternatively, a large group of people might split into smaller groups randomly.

The spoke's role is to relay information between the small group and the spokes council. The spoke needs to act as a voice for everyone within the small group, communicating the breadth of collective thought, rather than just their own personal point of view. Being the spoke carries a lot of responsibility to represent information accurately and not to manipulate the process.

Generally, spokes don't make decisions for their group, but always check back for agreement before a decision is finalised. However, an individual small group may empower their spoke to make decisions within agreed parameters.

Rotating the role of spoke from meeting to meeting is a good idea, as is having two spokes, one of them presenting the viewpoints and proposals from their small group, the other to take notes of what other groups have to say. This helps to ensure that ideas don't get lost or misrepresented.

Why small groups? Some people don't see the need to split into small groups – they want to hear the whole discussion and have everyone else hear their point of view. However, large plenary meetings make it very difficult for everyone to participate. There's not enough time for everyone to speak and many people feel too intimidated to talk in front of hundreds of people. Breaking into small groups creates safer, more dynamic spaces to work in, includes more people and saves a lot of time. Small groups can also allow several tasks to be done in parallel.

CHAPTER SUMMARY

The key points of this chapter are:

- How to handle conflict and drive decisions making.
- The nature of group conflict is normal in groups and, often, conflict can be beneficial.

- The application of simple and proven conflict resolution techniques are illustrated and various strategies to drive the appropriate outcomes.
- A simple set of guidelines are set out for the less experienced facilitators before moving into getting the group to decisions and consensus.
- The key skills to pull off consensus using a simple guidelines.

Section III

Advanced Facilitation Skills and Methods

5

Understanding Groups and Individuals: Facilitating a Synergistic Dynamic

The world is moved not only by the mighty shoves of heroes, but also by the aggregate of the tiny pushes of each honest worker.

People doing the same thing in the best possible way doesn't necessarily result in group productivity. This is merely the duplication of work. It is when energies are spent cooperatively and collaboratively that productivity is maximised. This requires a skilled facilitator who can manage group activities in creative and dynamic ways. Synergistic facilitation helps create a dynamic where the diverse ideas and skills of group members blend and integrate into a meaningful, vigorous and constructive whole. As H.E. Luccock said, "No one can whistle a symphony. It takes a whole orchestra to play it." Facilitation is an art in itself and the masterful application of facilitation skills enables the facilitator to produce a glorious symphony of individual skills and efforts.

As a synergist, the facilitator aspires for the ideal or the best possible result of group work. It is expected that in group work one plus one plus one does not necessarily add up to three. Sometimes, the result may be zero – or even negative. Team effectiveness is besieged with several challenges that derail team processes and deter positive results. Being the process expert, a facilitator is in the unique position to bring about synergy so that the team may be able to produce outputs greater than the sum of their inputs. The facilitator is tasked to create a framework for the group activity that reduces process losses, maximises the potential outcomes and boosts process gains.

The simple equation: Potential Outcome – Process Loss = Actual Outcome is anchored on the Input–Process–Output idea where the quality or the amount of group output depends on how the input is processed such that potential group effectiveness is not always equal to actual group effectiveness.

$$PO - PL = AO$$

PO – Potential Outcome, PL – Process Loss, AO – Actual Outcome

The potential outcome of a group is defined by the inputs. The inputs relevant to the job of a facilitator include the following factors:

- Skills, knowledge and attitudes of group members.
- Group norms, values and characteristics.
- Existing relationships and interactions, such as authority and influence.
- Group size.
- Resources.
- Nature of task or purpose.
- Developmental phase.
- Reward structure.

How these inputs are processed will either increase or decrease team process losses. Some of the process variables include the following:

- Utilisation of resources.
- Use of skills and knowledge.
- Task performance strategies and tools.
- Communication structures.
- Work coordination.
- Atmosphere.

The facilitator could not change the inputs, as they are givens. It is the facilitator's responsibility to make sure that group interactions and processes optimise these givens and also make up for inadequacies, rectify errors and/or capitalise on emerging opportunities. In such cases, the team may be able to supersede expected performance. The actual output is not simply a document or a decision written on paper.

Group outcomes include the following:

- Task accomplishment.
- Quality of outcomes and decisions.
- Satisfaction and emotional tone.
- Social integration.

It is clear that the ability of the facilitator to minimise team process loss is dependent on how well he or she understands the nature of groups and group processes.

Later sections in this book elaborate on these concepts to give the facilitator a deeper understanding of groups. Examples of how these concepts are applied in the world of facilitation are given to amplify their significance.

DIMENSIONS OF GROUP INTERACTIONS AND RELATIONSHIPS

In order to set the stage for maximum participation and productivity, the facilitator should know what factors influence individuals and how they interact with other group members. Effective facilitation addresses these different dimensions (Figure 5.1).

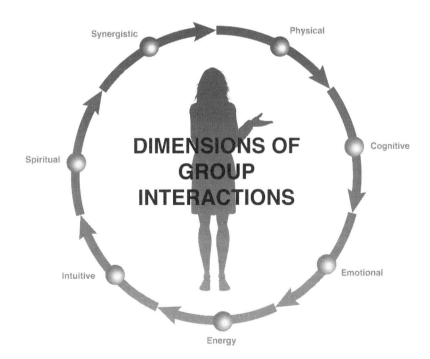

FIGURE 5.1
The dimensions of group interactions. (Adapted from Hunter, Bailey & Taylor, 1995.)

Physical dimension: The physical environment. The facilitator should focus on:

- Keeping members comfortable and safe.
- Attending to their physical needs to increase energy and productivity.
- Providing tools and resources for easier learning and doing.

Cognitive dimension: Existing knowledge and skills and the predominant cognitive/learning styles of the members. The facilitator should focus on:

- Emphasising the significance of the group activity to the member's welfare and development.
- Adopting a flexible strategy to cater to a range of experiences and cognitive preferences (see Learning Styles).
- Tapping the cognitive strengths of individuals to maximise their contribution (see Levels of Focus).
- Providing supplementary information or suggestions when appropriate.

Emotional dimension: Feelings, emotions, prejudices and dispositions of the members and also the emotions that the activity is likely to evoke. The facilitator should focus on:

- Fostering individual self-esteem.
- Respecting individual differences.
- Keeping in check any indication of emotional outburst.
- Instilling a sense of belonging.
- Maintaining confidentiality.
- Being authentic.

Energy dimension: The level of energy, interest and enthusiasm. The facilitator should focus on:

- Monitoring time and tasks to minimise delays and disruptions.
- Pacing and varying group activities interspersed with icebreakers to liven up energy.
- Helping members understand their role and the role of other team members.

- Setting and enforcing guidelines for interaction and encouraging the group to self-monitor.
- Giving praise where it is due and encouraging acknowledgement.

Intuitive dimension: Latent perceptions and feelings that are unexpressed or suppressed. The facilitator should focus on:

- Emphasising the value of open and clear communication.
- Being sensitive to unspoken ideas and emotions.
- Observing member and group behaviour for any indication of suppressed emotions.
- Listening.
- Drawing out members to voice their opinions and sentiments.
- Encouraging feedback.

Strategic dimension: The higher purpose of the group as well as of the individual members. The facilitator should focus on:

- Ensuring that the team adopts and understands a clearly defined, compelling goal or vision.
- Challenging the members to cooperate with the team in accomplishing the vision.
- Keeping the big picture in mind.

Synergistic dimension: The level of transformation and integration; maximising group dynamic and effectiveness. The facilitator should focus on:

- Ensuring acceptance and understanding of the group's decisions and output.
- Communicating and emphasising what needs to be done and how to do it, as has been agreed upon by the group.
- Creating buy-in.
- Focusing on results.
- Celebrating milestones and successes.

One dimension that needs to be pointed out is the interpersonal dimension. The type of group or the nature of the group purpose is a key factor which the facilitator considers in planning and managing the process.

The facilitator should balance task and maintenance roles to address the particular needs of the group. Some groups are organised around a cognitive agenda or a behavioural action agenda with less emphasis on emotional involvement. Other groups may need the integration of the cognitive, emotional and spiritual dimensions. Regardless of group type, the facilitator should never lose sight of the transformative aspects.

CYCLES OF GROUP DEVELOPMENT

Developing work teams requires an understanding of their evolution from non-performing to high-performing groups. Facilitating a team means managing group process through its ups and, especially, through its downs.

Familiarity with the dynamics of interactions, behaviours, level of morale and focus in each stage of development helps the facilitator in anticipating problems and opportunities to give support and to elevate the team to the next phase.

One of the most widely used models in describing the life cycles of teams is Tuckman's (1965) "Orming" model which consists of four stages: forming, storming, norming and performing. Tuckman belatedly added a fifth stage of the group life cycle – adjourning (Tables 5.1 and 5.2; Figure 5.2).

TABLE 5.1

Facilitator Involvement in the Tuckman Model

Stage	Level of morale	Productivity	Dependence on facilitator	Facilitator involvement
FORMING Embryonic stage	High	Low	High	High
STORMING Conflict stage	Low	Slowly increasing	High but decreasing	High but decreasing
NORMING Integration stage	Medium/high	Significantly increasing	Still decreasing	Decreasing
PERFORMING Synergistic stage	High	High	Low	Low
UNFORMING Dissolution stage	Depends on group outcome	Low	Low	Low

Adapted from Tuckman (1965).

TABLE 5.2

Facilitation Focus through the Team Development Phases

Dominant attitudes and behaviours	Major challenges	Facilitation focus
FORMING		
Excitement	Dissonance	Organisation and
Positive outlook	Unfamiliarity with other	control
Pride	members	Exploration of goals,
Tentativeness to participate	Lack of cooperation	roles, responsibilities
Politeness		and relevant
Concern about time requirements		procedures
		Discussion of concerns
		and expectations
STORMING		
Tension	Resistance to or	Reorienting focus
Hostility	changing attitudes	Conflict resolution
Defensiveness/guardedness	about team	Establishing
Discomfort	Dependence on other	cohesiveness
Competitiveness	group members	Providing facts or
Confusion	Processes often ignored	information to assist
		the team in making a
		decision
		Motivation
NORMING		
Relief	Reduced participation	Open communication
Committed	Misconceptions	Consensus building
Team cohesion/unity		Focus/refocus
Acceptance of rules and roles		Feedback
Tolerance		Instil accountability
Respect		
PERFORMING		
Understanding	Dwindling enthusiasm	Collaboration
Satisfaction with progress	Lack of focus	Provision of resources
Team spirit	Emergence of new	Evaluation of team
Active participation	problems and barriers	effectiveness
Independent worker	to task	Rewarding the team
	accomplishments	Adapting to change
	Lack of resources	
ADJOURNING		
Satisfaction	Lack of commitment to	Feedback
Constructive self-change	pursue decisions	Encouragement for
Separation anxiety		continued collaboration
		Praise/reward

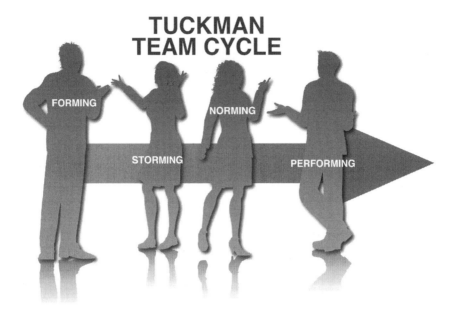

FIGURE 5.2
The Tuckman model of team development.

Forming

Forming is the stage where people are still working as individuals and they have just come together to be acquainted and to form as a group. It is here where they start exploring *why* they are forming as a group. Forming entails the development of group identity and commitment and seeking structure and direction. Individuals are concerned about acceptance and inclusion.

Storming

Storming is the stage of conflict. Members become more oriented with how they will work with each other, but there is still no discernible group structure giving rise to conflicts and loss of enthusiasm. With the emerging issues of power and control, individuals are concerned about autonomy, dependency and self-assertion.

Norming

Norming is the calm after the storm. It is the period of relief after control concerns have been threshed out. To norm means to resolve conflicts, establish rules and agree on the group's purpose. It is called the consolidating phase in which a group structure emerges, and the team determines how to use the resources they have to execute plans and achieve their higher purpose.

Performing

Performing is the synergistic stage in which the members are able to work as a team and to resolve emerging issues. There is productive collaboration as the group structure is more firmly established. Individuals are functioning interdependently towards the shared purpose.

Adjourning

"Unforming" or dissolution of the group. To unform means to let go of the group structure and move on to other tasks and responsibilities in the organisation. As the group progresses through these stages, the levels of morale and team effectiveness vary, so does the degree of facilitator involvement.

In the forming stage, although there is much excitement and positive expectations, the members are still in the process of getting oriented with the group's purpose and with knowing how to work with each other. Morale is high and productivity is low.

Hence, they are highly dependent on the facilitator to direct group processes so that they are able to clarify goals and expectations and build group connections.

In the storming stage, which is characterised by dissatisfaction, doubt and hostility, group morale is at its lowest. Team effectiveness is virtually nil, such that facilitation is much needed. The facilitator takes on a manager's role to ease out tension and resolve conflicts. In the norming stage, group morale and team effectiveness increase and the facilitator's involvement diminishes. The facilitator functions like a consultant, helping the group only when necessary.

In the performing stage, where group morale and productivity are at their highest, the facilitator gets involved only when it is necessary, such as when impending conflict becomes apparent. The facilitator takes on a supporting role to sustain group processes and prepares for closure and evaluation issues.

The progression of group development depicts how the facilitator interacts with the group as it evolves. As the group matures, norms and relationships are established, and the facilitator adapts to these intra-group changes.

The facilitator's task differs in each of the stages. Knowing the particular group and individual behaviours in each stage guides the facilitator in preparing facilitation activities.

ADULT LEARNING STYLES

Group members bring to the team not just a diverse set of perceptions, emotions and skills, but also different styles of learning and doing. The members of a team – although they may have similar concerns or functions – come into the group with their own distinctive way of approaching ideas and experiences. Understanding the characteristics of various types of adult learners will guide the facilitator in designing facilitation strategies that cut across a variety of learning preferences.

Two of the most widely used descriptions of the learning process are Kolb's model of experiential learning and Honey and Mumford's learning cycle.

Kolb's Learning Styles

David Kolb's (1984) experiential learning theory proposes that learning is a product of the processing or the transformation of experience. Put simply, a given learning style is shaped by the interaction between people and their environment.

Learners have two preferred methods to deal with experience:

- Concreteness or Abstractness.
- Activity or Reflection.

Concreteness involves feeling, while Abstractness involves thinking. Activity entails doing, while Reflection entails watching. Kolb argues that the learning process engages these four modes in a cyclical fashion. As such, learners may enter the learning cycle at any point depending on the circumstances. People apply these four processes in learning, but individuals are more inclined to gravitate towards one particular learning mode, more so than another (Figure 5.3). A typical illustration of Kolb's learning models shows two continuums, along two axes.

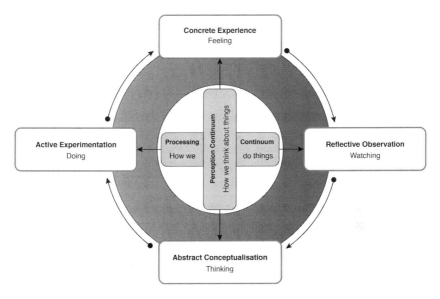

FIGURE 5.3
The matrix of experimental learning.

The vertical dimension is the perception continuum where the learners have a preference between learning by feeling or thinking.

- In the **Feeling (Concrete Experience – CE)** dimension, as learners encounter a new event or re-encounter an existing experience, they perceive these things or specific events as they are.
- In the **Thinking (Abstract Conceptualisation – AC)** dimension, the learners perceive things as concepts and ideas which lead them to analyse and understand the situation and to create new abstract concepts or modify existing ones.

The horizontal dimension is the processing continuum which depicts the preferred approach to a task, whether they opt to learn by watching or by doing.

- In the **Watching (Reflective Observation – RO)** dimension, learners observe and reflect on the new idea or experience before making a judgement.
- In the **Doing (Active Experimentation – AE)** dimension, learners apply what they have concluded and see whether it works, leading to new ideas, conclusions and experience.

To give a simple illustration of Kolb's learning cycle, let us take a person who is learning how to facilitate. In *concrete experience*, the learner may be trained by a coach who teaches how to facilitate. In abstract conceptualisation, the learner reads books and pamphlets to understand the principles of facilitation and how to plan a facilitation process. In reflective observation, the learner observes how experienced facilitators do their job and reflects on the applicability of theories he or she has read. In *active experimentation*, the learner serves as a co-facilitator to apply what he or she has decided to be their facilitation style and to discover if their techniques are effective.

The social environment, life experiences and, perhaps, even the cognitive structure of the learner shapes their learning preferences. These preferences are on one end of each continuum, representing what Kolb calls "dialectically related modes" of "grasping experience" (doing or watching) and "transforming experience" (feeling or thinking). A more elaborate illustration of these continuums shows the resulting learning preferences. Each quadrant shows the combination of variables or the combination of choices from perceiving and processing dimensions which then defines learning style (Figure 5.4).

Each quadrant represents a particular learning style.

- **Diverging** (concrete/reflective) – a *diverger* is both a concrete experiencer and a reflective observer.
- **Assimilating** (abstract/reflective) – an *assimilator* is both an abstract conceptualiser and a reflective observer.
- **Converging** (abstract/active) – a *converger* is both an abstract conceptualiser and an active experimenter.
- **Accommodating** (concrete/active) – an *accommodator* is both a concrete experiencer and an active experimenter.

FIGURE 5.4
Kolb's learning styles.

So how exactly do these different learner types think, feel and do things? Although they have similarities, there are many marked differences.

Divergers (the "why" learners):

- Watch rather than do.
- Possess imaginative ability as a key strength.
- Prefer gathering information, interpreting experiences and creating multiple perspectives.
- Perform better with innovative and imaginative approaches to doing things.
- Learn better through discussion, logical instruction or experimentation with instruction.
- Are interested in people and enjoy working with others.
- Have open minds and welcome feedback.
- Dislike time limits, conflict, task-oriented activities, being coached, unorganised learning structures.

Assimilators (the "what" learners):

- Think rather than do.
- Possess theory-building as a key strength.
- Prefer abstract thinking and deductive reasoning rather than social interaction; logically sound theories rather than practical value.
- Perform better with logical and thoughtful approaches to allow organised and structured understanding.
- Learn better through analytical instruction, lecture-demonstration, explanation and integration of high-level concepts.
- Place greater importance on ideas and abstract concepts than on people.
- Are partial to the opinions of experts.
- Prefer project designing, experimentation/exploration, lectures and independent reading.
- Dislike unorganised information, criticism, emotional appeal, unclear procedures and ambiguity.

Convergers (the "how" learners):

- Do rather than think.
- Possess practical application as a key strength.
- Prefer decision-making, problem-solving and the practical application of concepts and theories.

- Perform better in technical approaches and independent work.
- Learn better with interactive approaches that utilise simulation, experimentation and practical applications.
- Place greater importance on technical problems and tasks than on interpersonal connections.
- Are partial to facts rather than ideas or opinions.
- Prefer computer-based learning and experiments.
- Dislike large group activities, lectures, talking about feelings and theoretical discussions.

Accommodators (the "what if" and "why not" learners):

- Do rather than think/reflect.
- Possess task performance as a key strength.
- Prefer flexible and intuitive style rather than fact-finding and logical analysis.
- Perform better in hands-on and trial-and-error approaches.
- Learn better in practical and experiential activities, such as discovery learning.
- Place greater importance on new challenges and experiences rather than on reason and routine.
- Tend to be at ease with people.
- Prefer hands-on experiments and practical learning.
- Dislike formality, silence, rigid routines and time-based agendas.

Honey and Mumford's Learning Cycle

Honey and Mumford's (2000) model of learning is largely based on Kolb's model. Despite there being many similarities, there are a few notable differences. For example, Honey and Mumford conclude that learning style is not static or locked. Rather, learners shift from one style to another depending on certain factors, such as depth of experience (Figure 5.5).

The cycle consists of the following four stages:

1. **Activity**: Having experience.
2. **Reflection**: Reviewing the experience.
3. **Theory**: Concluding from the experience to create theoretical ideas.
4. **Pragmatism**: Putting theory to practice.

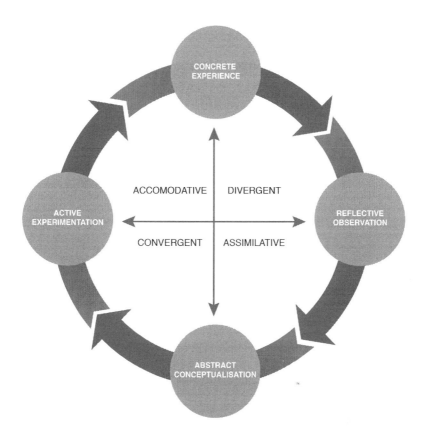

FIGURE 5.5
The learning cycles (Honey and Mumford).

In this cycle, learners can move in and out of quadrants. Put simply, learners can adopt a different learning style when unsuccessful, until they find the effective mode, and then jump out of the cycle when learning is successful.

Based on their model, Honey and Mumford proposed four learning styles, which share a number of similarities with Kolb's taxonomy:

Reflectors (the imaginative learners):

- Like to watch, think and review what is happening.
- Consider multiple viewpoints and all possible perspectives prior to decision-making.
- Prefer to study data and research.
- Prefer expert explanations and analysis.
- Prefer non-leader roles.

Theorists (the analytical learners):

- Like step-by-step and logical approaches to problem-solving.
- Prefer observing, analysing, synthesising and integrating concepts.
- Love asking questions.
- Prefer organised activities that have clear structures and objectives.

Pragmatists (the practical learners):

- Like to apply concepts and theories into actual practice.
- Prefer task-oriented activities and practical application.
- Put more importance on immediate use and practicality than on stretched observation and reflection.
- Enjoy making practical decisions and solving problems.

Activists (the dynamic learners):

- Enjoy the excitement and challenges of new experiences.
- Prefer experimentation and role-playing.
- Are comfortable with people and can assume leader or initiating roles.
- Are quick thinkers and decision-makers.
- Enjoy participating and having fun.

Members of facilitated groups will have a wide variety of learning preferences, yet will also favour a variety of group activities. It is much better if the facilitator is able to identify the dominant learning modality of the client group to be able to prepare a customised facilitation program.

In large groups however, an evaluation would be time-consuming and impractical. As some experts argue, learners frequently jump from one learning style to another, depending on their needs. It is therefore safe to assume that most of these learning styles are present and, as such, a balanced approach is reasonable. This balanced approach incorporates a diversity of learning styles that appeal to different kinds of learners and help them get the most out of their group experience.

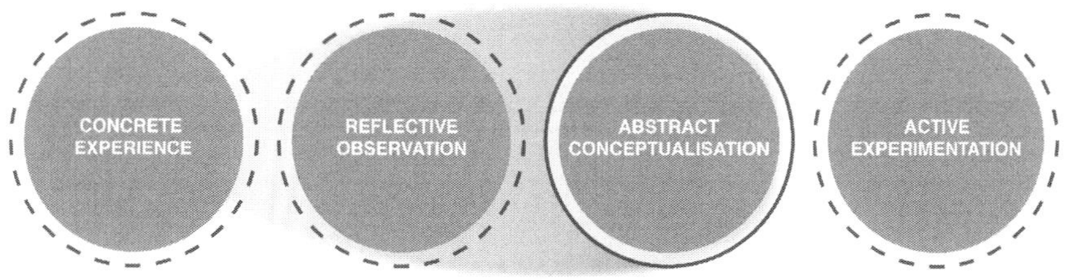

FIGURE 5.6
Frames of focus in learning cycles.

In designing a robust facilitation plan, the facilitator should take into consideration the four basic learning styles. A coherent approach would be to observe the cyclical stages in a logical fashion, starting from defining the purpose. Ask *why* the group is there. Next, ask what the task or topic is all about. Then, move on to exploring the *hows* and finally, to integrate the theories to answer the *ifs* (Figure 5.6).

This is especially applicable in skills training or knowledge building. The way to do this would look something like Table 5.3.

More importantly, you should be able to motivate each individual to feel a sense of ownership for what they have learned. I have listed some tools and techniques that would be appropriate for each learner type.

Reflectors/Divergers ("Why?" thinkers)

- Brainstorming.
- Paired discussion.
- Cooperative groups.
- Logs and journals.
- Self-reflection exercises.
- Observation.
- Questionnaires.
- Interviews simulation.

Assimilators/Theorists ("What?" thinkers)

- Readings.
- Lecture method/Direct instruction.
- Project designing.
- Experiments and hands-on exercises with lecture or explanation.
- Drill.

TABLE 5.3

Six-Step Facilitator Involvement

Activity	Learner activities	Facilitator focus

Step 1
Pre-work
"Where are we?"
	• Question and answer – learners share their previous knowledge.	• Review prior knowledge and experience.
		• Determine knowledge/skill level.
		• Watch out for misconceptions.
		• Present overview of session.
		• Explain activities.
		• Prepare supplies and materials:
		  • Textual aids.
		  • Multimedia charts, handouts, PowerPoint and other instructional aids.

Step 2 Exploration (Doing) "What/How is"	• Role-playing or simulations. • Demonstration. • Presentation. • Problem-solving. • Games. • Product exploration and/or designing. • Lab work. • Field trip. • Project-making.	• Ensure that activities to be performed by participants involve actual doing or performing. • Act as a guide only. • Answer clarifying questions on process or mechanics only. • Supplement activity tools when necessary – journals, workbooks, etc.

Step 3
Sharing
"What happened?"
	• (Free) public discussion.
	• Talk about experience.
	• Share reactions and observations.
	• Discuss feelings generated by experience.
		• Ensure maximum participation.
		• Guide questions:
		  • *What did you do?*
		  • *What happened?*
		  • *What did you see, feel, hear, taste?*
		  • *What were the specific skills you used to complete the task?*
		  • *What was the most difficult? Easiest?*
		  • *What was the best/worst/ most challenging thing that happened?*

Step 4
Processing
"What's important?"
	• Reflect upon and analyse the experience.
	• Discuss how the experience was carried out.
	• Discuss how themes, problems and issues are brought by the experience.
		• Encourage the group to look for recurring themes.
		• Guide questions:
		  • *What problems or issues seemed to occur over and over?*
		  • *What are the things that we can agree on?*

(Continued)

TABLE 5.3 (CONTINUED)

Six-Step Facilitator Involvement

Activity	Learner activities	Facilitator focus
		• *Name three things that stuck in your mind about the activity.* • *What similar experience(s) have you had?* • *Did you notice any pattern in completing the task?*

Step 5
Generalising
"So what?"
	• Connect the experience with real-world examples (job, social life, etc.).
	• Pinpoint trends and common truths in the experience.
	• Identify "real-life" principles that emerged.
		• List (or have one participant write on the board) key terms that capture the activity.
		• Guide questions:
		  • *What have you learned about yourself through this activity?*
		  • *Why is this skill/knowledge important in your daily life?*
		  • *What impact does it have in your work, if any?*
		  • *How does what you learned relate to other parts of your life?*
		  • *What connections do you see between this lesson and your past experiences?*

Step 6
Application
"Now what?"
	• Identify real-life situations where the new learning could be applied.
	• Discuss how more effective behaviours can develop from the new learning.
	• Present how the lesson may be applied to future activities at work and at home.
		• If a lesson is more related to job performance, encourage them to cite specific examples.
		• Guide questions:
		  • *How can you apply what you learned to a new situation?*
		  • *How will you act differently in the future?*
		  • *What would need to change in order to fit this new learning?*
		  • *How did this experience challenge your assumptions and stereotypes?*
		  • *How could you apply life skills learned through this practice in the future?*
		  • *Where do you go from here? What's the next step?*

The framework was adapted from University of California, Davis – UC Davis experiential learning website at www.experientiallearning.ucdavis.edu/module2/el2-40-5step-definitions.pdf, but modified to relegate the teacher to a facilitator role or process guide only.

Convergers/Pragmatists ("How?" thinkers)

- Practical applications.
- Simulations.
- Case studies.
- Interactive and hands-on instruction.
- Laboratory or fieldwork.
- Computer-assisted instruction.
- Workbooks.
- Case studies.
- Problem-solving.

Accommodators/Activists ("What if?"/ "Why not?"/ "What then?" thinkers)

- Laboratory work.
- Fieldwork.
- Videos.
- Brainstorming.
- Role-play.
- Competitions.
- Group work.

Kolb's experiential learning theory is particularly applicable to adult learning because it is learner-centred and it addresses the cognitive, emotional and physical aspects of the learner and, therefore, incorporates authentic and real-life context into the learning structure.

The Attention, Generation, Emotion and Spacing (AGES) Model

It turns out that some of our long-held beliefs about learning are incorrect. For example, the importance of repetition in learning has proved to be not nearly as important as first thought. Likewise, while most educators believe that concentrated learning in one block of information at a time is most effective, neuroscience research is clearly showing that it is far better to break up learning interventions for a greater degree of successful, long-term information retention.

These recent discoveries are important in business as well. Amplified organisational change is increasing pressure on learning. Business and/ or organisational men and women are pressured to learn more, faster

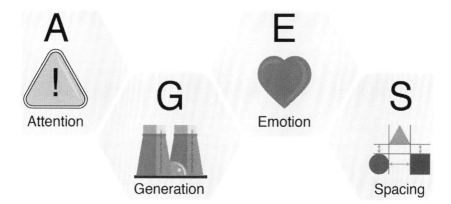

FIGURE 5.7
AGES model (David Rock).

and under tougher conditions – and within tighter budgets. With a firm understanding of how people learn, the facilitator will be in a better position to *facilitate* the agreed outcomes and solutions of their sessions (Figure 5.7).

In the workplace, much learning is declarative, or explicit learning, meaning information that needs to be recalled (Poldrack, Wagner, Davachi, & Dobbins, 2008). This kind of learning involves encoding information in the brain sufficiently well for easy retrieval. In any learning experience, whether learning a new product description or organisational chart, a key outcome of the experience is that information is remembered and can be recalled easily. Neuroscientists have discovered that the level of activation of a brain region called the hippocampus during an encoding task plays a significant role in whether people can recall what they learned (Davachi & Wagner, 2002).

These recent findings have been drawn together into one, easy-to-remember model, called AGES: Attention, Generation, Emotion and Spacing.

Attention

For the hippocampus to activate sufficiently for learning to occur, the learner needs to be paying full attention to the topic being learned. To that end, one of the foundational ideas for learning is ensuring you have "undivided attention" – that people are focused closely on the learning task at hand.

The facilitator must ensure that the group is focused at all times during the sessions. It may be helpful to:

- Turn off all mobile phones.
- Ensure everyone is familiar with the rules established for listening, talking, having breaks, etc.
- Keep the energy in the room relevant, high and focused.
- Keep speeches short and succinct.
- Create an overall environment that is relaxed and comfortable.
- Have regular, short breaks.
- Avoid scheduling sessions that clash with events to which some people's attention will be naturally drawn (like grand finals, elections, etc.).
- Ensure everyone in the group is involved, not just a small portion – leaving the others to be easily distracted.

Generation

The manner in which the human brain *generates* the memories of what it has learned is directly related to how well the individual can retrieve the learned information at a later stage. Both psychological and neuroscientific research shows that the key to optimising learning and building long-term memory is to create "ownership" of learning content (Jensen, 2005; Poldrack et al., 2001). It is important, therefore, for learners to transform the information before them into something that is relevant to them and/ or their business or organisation.

This is similar to the feature/benefits paradigm in sales. Customers don't particularly care for the technical particulars of a selected product (the *feature*), but by describing how that feature transforms into something beneficial for the customer (the *benefit*), not only will the customer gain a greater understanding of the product, but they will be better placed to make judgements and decisions pertaining to the product. Put simply, they will "remember" the product and its benefits.

In facilitation sessions therefore, the facilitator must do all he or she can to ensure that the information being shared throughout the group is given the opportunity to be interpreted – or *transformed* – by the individual participants as to how it best impacts their path to the agreed solutions and outcomes. This can be achieved through discussion or through challenging individual members to identify how the relevant information is important to them. Questioning the learner triggers retrieval of recently learned information and improves long-term retention.

Emotions

Learning happens in many complex layers, with emotion being one of the more important regulators of learning and memory formation. Studies show that the correlation of vividness of a memory and the emotionality of the original event is around 0.9 (Jensen, 2005).

The way in which emotion is thought to enhance memory is twofold. First, emotional content is thought to grab the attention of the individual and, hence, helps to focus attention on the emotional event or stimulus (LeDoux, 1994; Damasio, 1994). Second, it is known that emotion leads to the activation of a brain structure called the amygdala which sits directly in front of the hippocampus and can help to signal to the hippocampus that a particular event is salient, and thus increases the effectiveness of encoding (Ochsner, 2000; Cahill et al., 1994).

Generating strong negative emotions in a training program, such as fear, is a commonly used strategy for burning memories. For example, many sales, presentation and negotiation programs are based on videotaped sessions, which focus on the negatives of the presenter instead of their strengths.

However, there are difficulties with using strong negative emotions to burn in memories: negative emotions also reduce creativity and innovation (Subramaniam et al., 2009), so while people may learn, they are less likely to innovate. Also, the brain's organising principle is to minimise threat and maximise reward (Gordon, 2000). As a result, people are not going to be inclined to turn up for training when the experience continues to use negative emotions, and they are likely to warn their colleagues to stay away too. However, if a learning experience is fun, they are likely to want to do more learning and tell others about the positive event.

To maximise the retention of knowledge during a session, the facilitator must remain consciously vigilant about the emotional needs of the participants. The facilitator should ensure that:

- The environment in which the session is taking place is relaxed and comfortable.
- The participants are individually respected and the session overall is a *safe* environment, promoting a willingness for their emotions to be more openly accessible.

- A general ambience of fun and enjoyment is present throughout the session.
- All participants are encouraged to share their thoughts, feelings and emotions during the session.

Spacing

It has been known for some time that distributing learning over time is better than cramming learning into one long study session (Crowder, 1976). Spacing of the learning process thus plays an important role in how well the information is retained. Spacing allows the brain to further digest new content and over time build and wire new connections, even when learners are at rest (Spitzer, 2002; Tambini et al., 2010). Spacing enhances memory performance and the rate of forgetting drops due to enhanced hippocampally mediated memory consolidation (Litman & Davachi, 2008).

The facilitator should avoid "cramming" the session with too much information, because key points will be lost among the participants. While always under the constraint of time and budget, it would be a false economy to try and *squeeze* content into an unrealistic timeframe simply to save money.

Brain function shows multiple constraints around learning limitations with regard to learning a lot of information, including:

- The limitations of the prefrontal cortex and its ability to process only three to seven information chunks at any one time (Linden et al., 2003).
- The time necessary to form new synaptic connections (Goda & Davis, 2003).
- If the synapse gets disturbed before it "sets", the memory is lost (Milner, 1999).
- The "rest-time" needed to allow the brain to recycle protein in the neurons, which is crucial for building long-term memory (Bodizs et al., 2002; Schroth, 2002).
- The "digestion-time" needed for the brain to reorganise, distribute and consolidate new content through the hippocampus (Piegneux et al., 2001; Stickgold, 1998; Siapas & Wilson, 1994; Walker & Stickgold 2006) and awake rested (Tambini et al., 2010).

Facilitators must ensure each session is appropriately balanced between the amount of information being shared and the time for the participants to absorb, process and understand the information. One way for the facilitator to achieve this is to impart small amounts of information, and then revisit the information after a short break, either through discussion, analyses or both. There is evidence that initial testing of newly learned items, with a small delay after the learning event, will further drive the building of long-term memory, as this causes an additional retrieval effort (Karpicke & Roediger, 2007).

Adult learning is highly complex. How do we ensure people are interested in learning what is presented, and how then do we present the information to ensure that the knowledge is sustainable, accessible and easily applied in adaptive and contextual ways?

To these ends, facilitators should focus on:

- Creating maximum **attention** with a greater focus on learner motivation, ensuring one focus during learning events and utilising more novelty and change during learning experiences.
- Encouraging significant **generation** of learning by participants when teaching new concepts to build learner ownership, rather than using the presentation of information.
- Creating a positive **emotional** environment with opportunities for people to gain positive feedback and connect deeply with others.
- Utilising more **spacing** of learning instead of massing and repetition, with more dispersed content, such as turning a three-day learning event into six half-day events over a longer period.

PRINCIPLES OF ADULT LEARNING

In addition to these learning cycles and models, facilitators should also consider some particular characteristics of adult learners. Adult learners are different from young learners in many ways. First, they come into a session with years of life experience and well-formed beliefs and expectations. They have preconceived notions of what learning is like, such that they are quick to refute anything that is against their beliefs and values. They have responsibilities (home, family, work, etc.) and issues (problem children, marital issues, low income, amortisations, etc.). Adults have also experienced biological changes, for example, a decrease in memory.

Georgi Lozanov, a Bulgarian educator and psychiatrist, in his ground-breaking theory of adult learning, proposed that all adults have core thinking reserves deep within their brains and that these reserves can be harnessed to enhance learning once learning becomes a pleasurable experience.

Powerful learning engages both the analytical brain and the emotional brain, such that learning is best in a climate that evokes positive emotions, celebrates learning and inspires a feeling of possibilities within the learner (International Alliance for Learning).

Adult learners come into the learning process with their own beliefs and mental models about themselves, the world, the subject matter and learning itself.

The facilitator's role is to support the learner in becoming aware of these beliefs through a combination of subtle questions and a rich variety of learning tasks and processes. Drawing on the two words "suggestion" and "pedagogy", Lozanov called his theory "Suggestopedia". The term has since been modified to "accelerated learning".

In summary, there are four key principles of *Suggestopedia* that are relevant to adult learning:

1. A facilitator is more effective than a lecturer or instructor.
2. All the elements in the learning environment either promote or hinder learning.
3. Active engagement and participation in the learning process enhances learning.
4. The use of the arts (such as music, acting, drawing and visuals) reaches past the logical components of the human brain into the deeper and emotive core.

To know more on psychological models, see Chapter 3, Ladder of Inference.

Table 5.4 illustrates how the facilitator can apply these principles in order to maximise adult learning.

Theories in multimedia learning also support the value of presenting a wide variety of media. Garr (2010) cites three basic assumptions in how the brain processes information:

TABLE 5.4

Facilitating against the Adult Learning Principles

Principles of adult learning	Facilitator focus

Adults remember:
  10% of what they hear,
  65% of what they hear and see,
  80% of what they hear, see and do.
	• Introduce a combination of activities that stimulate aural, visual and audio-visual perception and that incorporate practical exercises.
	• Alternate materials and media for each activity to suit learning preference.

Adults are relevancy oriented. They need to feel that learning focuses on issues that directly concern them. The greater the degree of relevance (to personal life or to a job) to the individual, the greater is the degree of learning.	• Help them discover the link between what they are learning and their lives. • Amplify the importance of the topic or the task and how it applies to the learner's needs. • Show the relevance of the methods to their jobs. • Give concrete examples that are directly related to their work experience. • Integrate group learning activities that engage the members in making practical decisions and solving problems related to their jobs. • Conduct hands-on training or simulated activities if possible.
Adults need to be able to integrate new ideas into what they already know if they are going to be able to retain the information.	• Learn the level of knowledge and skills of the group members. • Involve adult learners in diagnosing their needs. • Draw on prior knowledge and experience and allow members to engage with new knowledge so that personal meaning can be created. • Present information or allow new knowledge to emerge or be presented in a logical manner. Be generous with practical examples that touch on their experiences. • Provide enough flexibility to allow student input in terms of content and learning process.
Adults are autonomous and self-directed. They prefer self-directed and self-paced instruction to group learning led by an instructor. Adults need to be actively involved in the learning process.	• Provide activities that allow for maximum participation. • Encourage participants to identify resources and devise appropriate strategies for using resources to achieve objectives. • Give the participants more control over their learning. Have them decide the progression of activities and make them understand their roles and responsibilities. • Enforce ground rules to keep the group on track and on time to avoid problems, such as social distraction. Review progress periodically. • If the training is done in a group led by the instructor, build in independent activities; consider trainee-focused approaches to training.

(Continued)

TABLE 5.4 (CONTINUED)

Facilitating against the Adult Learning Principles

Principles of adult learning	Facilitator focus
Adults bring a great deal of experience and learning history to training.	• Use good questioning skills to draw out adults to share their experiences, knowledge and skills. • Create curiosity, interest and energy by emphasising personal meaning and the value of social interaction. • Be sensitive to the motivations, moods and feelings of the group members. Protect minority opinion and make disagreements civil. • Ensure that learning materials and processes are attuned to the maturity level of the participants.
Adults are practical. They are goal oriented and need to see immediate application and validation of what they are learning. Integration of new knowledge and skills on the job requires application on the job.	• Conduct on-the-job training or simulated activities if possible. • Set the appropriate level of difficulty that challenges. • Incorporate creativity, but not be too challenging, which could threaten the participants. • Incorporate follow-up activities or action plans to be used on the job.
Adult learning is enhanced in an informal collaborative and respectful climate that allows democratic participation.	• Treat the participant as an equal. • Acknowledge individual differences. • Remind the group that criticisms should be constructive and should be directed to ideas and not to the person. • Establish learning groups based on preferences, skills, etc. Adults naturally radiate towards people with similar mindsets.
Adults need dialogue, engagement and social interaction.	Design learning structures that allow learners to collaborate with other people (cooperative groups, paired groups). Incorporate multiple methods of feedback.

Modified and adapted from A. F. Ittner, A. F. and P. L. *Train the Trainer*, 2nd ed., Human Resource Development Press, 1997; M. Knowles, *The Adult Learner: A Neglected Species*. Houston: Gulf Publishing, 1984; and Stephen Lieb, *Principles of Adult Learning*, VISION, Fall 1991.

1. **Dual channel** – visual and verbal materials are processed separately in different channels.
2. **Limited capacity** – each channel can only process a limited amount of information at a time.
3. **Active processing** – understanding of information is enhanced when relevant information is coherent and integrated with prior knowledge and experience.

The most important implication of these assumptions is that information presented to learners should be simple, coherent and compelling.

The facilitator should consider the following guidelines in preparing tools and techniques, as suggested by Garr (2010):

- Saying words is better than showing words (narration rather than showing text).
- Saying and showing/illustrating is better than simply saying it (narration plus pictures rather than narration only).
- Saying and illustrating is better than saying, illustrating and displaying the text (narration plus graphics rather than narration, graphics and text).
- Simple and clean is better than complex and cluttered (extraneous visual material is precisely that – extraneous).

The "Four-Quadrant" Opening: Motivating the Adult Learner

So what motivates adults to learn? According to Lieb (1991), there are six primary motivating factors of adult learners:

1. **Social relationships** – to make new friends and to meet a need for associations and friendships.
2. **External expectations** – to comply with instructions from someone else; to fulfil the expectations or recommendations of someone with formal authority.
3. **Social welfare** – to improve the ability to serve mankind, prepare for service to the community and improve the ability to participate in community work.
4. **Personal advancement** – to achieve higher status in a job, secure professional advancement and stay abreast of competitors.
5. **Escape/stimulation** – to relieve boredom, provide a break in the routine of home or work and provide a contrast to other exacting details of life.
6. **Cognitive interest** – to learn for the sake of learning, seek knowledge for its own sake and to satisfy an inquiring mind.

One effective way to motivate participants is to do the four-quadrant opening that addresses mutual concerns. Answering these questions shapes the proper mindset right at the start. Some of these issues will not become obviously clear to some, but motivation must be done at the beginning, not in the middle or when it's too late (Figure 5.8).

FIGURE 5.8
The four quadrants of participants.

At the start of the session, if the participants have an idea of why they are there, what sort of things they will do, what they will gain and how and where they are going to use their learning from the activity, then they are most likely to be motivated to learn.

The "**Why am I here?**" quadrant is answered by identifying the purpose of the activity.

The "**What will I get?**" quadrant can be explicitly – or implicitly – answered in the following ways:

- Emphasise how personal advancement could be achieved.
- Inspire with noble goals.
- State the overall purpose of the organisation.
- Offer a rationale of why the task is necessary.

Design activities that catch their interest and allow them to work with people. Let them have fun while working.

- Stir up conversations that satisfy their inquisitive nature and personal challenge.
- Infuse autonomy and flexibility.

The "**How will this work?**" quadrant gives them the overall map but not the specific ways to travel. Adult learners become more creative when they are not dictated to about *how* to do things.

Instead, the facilitator should merely state the general objective, then encourage the participants to identify specific ways of achieving the purpose and finally allow them freedom over how they act on their decisions.

In short, to engage them creatively, make them players not pawns. Let them draw up their boundaries. As the renowned author and blogger Seth Godin suggested:

> As an entrepreneur, I'm blessed with 100% autonomy over task, time, technique and team. Here's the thing: If I maintain that autonomy, I fail. I fail to ship. I fail to excel. I fail to focus. I inevitably end up either with no product or a product the market rejects. The art of the art is picking your limits. That's the autonomy I most cherish. The freedom to pick my boundaries.

And finally, the "**So what?**" quadrant. The underlying spirit of any subject is what's important to the individual. Once the learner grasps that, and really feels it within their whole being, learning becomes meaningful.

LEVELS OF FOCUS

All of us have, at some point in our lives, sat through a meeting that has dragged on and on, with intermittent emotional outbursts, doors slamming or fists pounding, people whispering in one corner or going in and out of the meeting place.

Or perhaps, we have attended a training session where the goals are unclear and the activities are in disarray, such that after a few hours, the trainees have not yet opened page one of their workbooks. In such instances, the groups have no focus or have lost focus. Either no one was acting as a facilitator or the facilitator was incompetent and rendered ineffective.

Rock (2007) suggests that individual participants (or the group as a whole) may find themselves at five different levels of focus: Vision, Planning, Detail, Problem and Drama. These five levels of focus also characterise five levels of thinking (Figure 5.9).

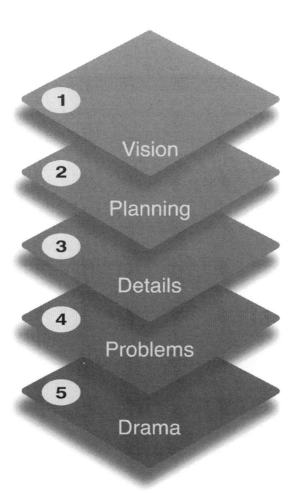

FIGURE 5.9
Levels of Focus (David Rock, 2008).

Sometimes, groups get hopelessly trapped in the levels below the dotted line and find it difficult – sometimes subconsciously – to shift gears and move to other levels of focus. It is not the case that *problem* and *drama* have an adverse effect on group effectiveness, it is getting *stuck* that is.

Analogously, it is a "sink or swim" situation. Staying under the dotted line or under the "waterline", the group drowns. Floating above the waterline, the group succeeds. The facilitator should enable the group to get past the drama and over-thinking of the problem and sway them to the other, more important, points of focus. The facilitator should identify the problem-focused or the drama-focused participants and identify ways to channel their energies towards productive efforts.

Vision

Aim

Formulate and decide on a common and binding purpose (broad and meaningful, but not detailed).

Challenges

- Members who tend to dwell too much on envisioning.
- Lack of agreement on the purpose.
- Too broad and vague or unrealistic an objective.
- Formation of cliques or subgroups.

Opportunities

- Visionary leaders who are adept in visualising the future and capturing the "big picture".
- Group expectations as a source of inspiration and cooperation.

Facilitator Focus

- Ask exploratory questions about what the group wants to achieve and why and what the measures of success are.
- Elicit a sense of purpose from the group and instil a sense of identity.
- Encourage the visionaries to articulate the agreed objective in meaningful and emotive words.
- Ensure that participants agree on the purpose of the group.

Planning

Aim

- Draw up a strategic plan (specific but not detailed) to achieve the group's vision.

Challenges

- Formulated strategies are beyond the capabilities of the group.
- Strategic plan is inadequate.
- Lack of confidence in the ability of the group.

Opportunities

- Energy is high.
- Presence of process and operation specialists among the members who could adeptly visualise the way forward.

Facilitator Focus

- Utilise helpful tools such as Gantt charts and flowcharts to enable members to visualise the plan.
- Use brainstorming and other group discussion techniques to elicit maximum participation.
- Ensure that the plans are essential to the overall vision.
- Observe "chunking" if the project is big.

Details

Aim

- Design the action plan, steps and timeline to carry out the strategy including role assignments and specific solutions.

Challenges

- Too much attention to detail.
- Analysis paralysis.
- Outlined tasks do not address the overall strategy.

Opportunities

- Energy and enthusiasm are high.
- Opportunities for individual members to find their niche.

Facilitator Focus

- Remind the group of the task schedule.
- Use creativity techniques to exhaust the best possible options and actions.
- Make a formal or informal survey of individual skills to determine role compatibilities.

Problems

Aim

- Identify problems and risks.

Challenges

- Defensive behaviours.
- Members who are too focused on thinking about problems, rather than finding solutions.
- Loss of confidence in the group's ability to accomplish its purpose.

Opportunities

- Members who are able to identify risks and weigh the pros and cons of decisions.

Facilitator Focus

- Tackle problems from a vision perspective or planning perspective.
- Assign the problem-focused team members as risk-assessors and give them time (but not too much) to contribute meaningfully, such as suggesting ways to manage the risks identified.
- Focus on the items that are agreed on (rather than attempting to agree on problems) to work towards visions.

Drama

Aim

- None (except maybe to derail the proceedings).

Challenges

- Emotionally charged atmosphere.
- Lack of reason and purpose.

Opportunities

- High energy.
- Emotional involvement is a form of participation.

Facilitator Focus

- Have the group get out of this focus immediately.
- Make them aware that the progress of the group is being derailed by unnecessary emotions and conflicts.
- Enforce ground rules.
- Identify disrupters and destructive behaviours and employ appropriate strategies to address these problems.
- Build group rapport.
- Use icebreakers to douse hot tempers and revive enthusiasm (the icebreaker may use content that is relevant to the reason for drama and conflict).

There will always be people who are focused on problems and drama, but there will also be members who are naturals in visioning, planning and execution. It is up to the facilitator to manage problematic and dramatic atmospheres for members to channel their energies to focusing on strengths and similarities, rather than on weaknesses and differences. Facilitators should be quick to identify members who are on different levels of focus but could complement each other. For example, organise small groups or paired groups with a vision-focused member and a drama-focused member so that the visionary may inspire the problem-oriented member to believe in the team's capability. A problem-focused member would work well with a planning-focused member – one identifies the dangers, the other responds with strategies to address these risks.

The recommended facilitator tasks are given merely as examples. There are many more strategies available to the facilitator contained in other sections of this book, for example, the use of excellent and timely questions.

You should remember that everything you do (and anything you fail to do) has an effect on the group dynamic. There is no set recipe or a guaranteed formula for synergistic facilitation. There are no hard and fast rules, but certainly, through practice and drawing from intuitive experience, the facilitator could be able to concoct a right mix of technical know-how and behavioural skills to build the foundation for synergy. The principles of group dynamics have been discussed in this chapter. The next chapters will present principles that could enhance one's behavioural skills and technical expertise. Conflicts and conflict resolution are discussed in a separate chapter.

TABLE 5.5

Hand Hints from the Zen of Groups

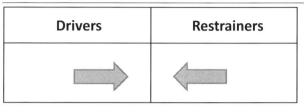

Drivers	Restrainers

I have selected some helpful tips from the book *The Zen of Groups: A Handbook for People Meeting with a Purpose* (Hunter, Bailey & Taylor, 1995) as a starter (Table 5.5).

THE CARER MODEL

The CARER model is a paradigm of intrinsic human behaviours that improves people's capacity to identify and understand – and ultimately, modify – their own and other people's behaviour in social situations to subsequently adapt those behaviours to be more conducive to the particular setting. In facilitation, the CARER model serves as a powerful tool not only for the facilitator to identify, modulate and progress his or her own behaviour during a facilitation session, but also, and perhaps more importantly, to recognise, shape and evolve the behaviour of the participants in the facilitation in order to guide them to a more successful outcome or solution.

Having a model to be able to better predict how people are likely to respond to change can serve to modify a potential threat into a potential. Neuroscience reveals that at least five human motivational needs require consideration and meeting in order to minimise threat and maximise reward. The importance of each of these needs will vary between individuals and may differ from situation to situation. For example, the need for a high level of certainty about your job, as compared with the unpredictability of a high-risk sporting activity in your leisure time.

The CARER model, adapted from SCARF (Rock, 2008), is underscored by a mindset of self-awareness and awareness of others, and a leadership identity as a CARER, rather than a "scarer"! (Figure 5.10).

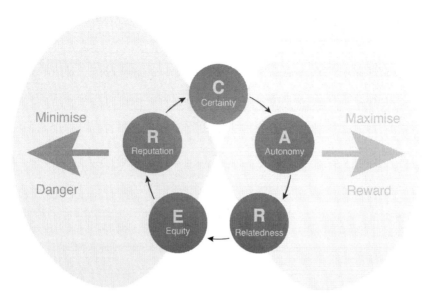

FIGURE 5.10
CARER model (J. Pratlett).

Since 2008, when the SCARF model was first proposed, advances in social neuroscience research have supported the basic tenets of the CARER model: the view that social concerns are a primary motivator for human behaviour, and that the human brain is primed to attend to and process social information in a privileged manner – when greater activity is stimulated in the brain regions that process reward and social information, social winning increases the likelihood that people will take more risks and be more competitive.

These and other social neuroscience findings conclude that the consideration of the social and emotional responses and needs of others play a vital role in helping people successfully collaborate and understand one another. This is especially relevant for individuals in a facilitator (or other leadership) role, since fostering and supporting rewarding experiences, such as the ownership of a solution by participants in a facilitation, is crucial for wellbeing, job satisfaction and overall organisational success.

While the topics covered thus far in this book are critically important for a successful facilitation session, the facilitator should always be consciously aware that it is the *social abilities* of members that drive performance and the motivation of seeking – and achieving – the agreed outcomes and solutions.

"Collective intelligence", or how well a group of people performs across a wide range of tasks, does not depend on how many smart people are in the group, but instead, is directly related to factors such as the social sensitivity of the group members and how much time is spent giving everyone in the group equal time to talk (Woolley, Chabris, Pentland, Hashmi, & Malone, 2010).

By familiarising themselves with the CARER model, the facilitator will be able to associate any of the CARER domains (or a combination of more than one working in combination) with their own feelings, actions and change, and with the contributions of the participants. The CARER model enables facilitators to be more adaptive by providing a clear, easy-to-remember language. Having this language improves our ability to label or reappraise our emotions, which helps to regulate social threats and rewards (Ochsner, 2008).

The CARER Model Explained

The following is a more detailed description of each of the five CARER domains and any facilitator who wishes to gain "an advantageous edge" should familiarise themselves with the CARER language. By doing so, the facilitator will be able to identify these paradigms in members participating in a facilitation and in him or herself.

Certainty (Predictable)

People differ in their need for certainty and their ability to tolerate uncertain or confusing situations. Specifically, intolerance of ambiguity is the tendency for a person to perceive confusing or uncertain situations as a threat. A person's ability to tolerate confusion has profound implications for whether or not uncertain social situations (such as addressing difficult and controversial organisational issues or having to work with a new team of people) will be met with adaptability or with overwhelming levels of anxiety and stress.

The effective facilitator must remain vigilantly aware of the uncertainty felt by participants in the facilitation, particularly in individuals or teams who are unfamiliar with each other, large groups (and the prospect of being broken out into spokes councils with possible unfamiliar members) and when facilitating executive teams (see Chapter 6) where ego, organisational restraint and expectation and personal agendas may play a larger role and could transform into a greater uncertainty for some members.

People generally need to be able to predict what's happening ahead of time. Familiar music is predictable, we anticipate what is coming next and the brain likes that certainty. Leaders can provide certainty by being transparent, providing updates on management decisions, being clear on their expectations and ensuring their team understand how their work contributes to the company's performance. In most situations, uncertainty creates a threat state.

Google's HR team had learned from their measuring management performance just how effective certainty, created by consistency:

> We found that, for leaders, it's important that people know you are con-sistent and fair in how you think about making decisions and that there's an element of predictability. If a leader is consistent, people on their teams experience tremendous freedom, because then they know that within cer-tain parameters, they can do whatever they want. If your manager is all over the place, you're never going to know what you can do, and you're going to experience it as very restrictive.

> *Laszlo Bock, Human Resource Executive* **(Bryant, 2013)**

Take an organisational restructure, for example, people need to know what's going on. It is important to give people even a small amount of certainty, such as, "I'll get back to you tomorrow morning at nine." Even if by 9:00 am you have no news, letting people know that gives them more certainty than saying, "I don't know anything, but I'll let you know when I know something." It lets them at least think, "My manager will update me tomorrow. I can let that worry go for now."

Kevin Rudd announced on 8 July 2013 proposed changes to rules to allow all Labour party members a vote to determine the leader of their party. "Today, more than ever, Australians demand to know that the prime minister they elected, is the prime minister they get. The Australian public requires that certainty. These changes will give them that certainty." (In the process increasing his level of certainty too, no doubt.)

Be clear, reassuring, routine, consistent, predictable, regular, transparent, honest and reliable.

Autonomy (Discretion)

People have a fundamental need for personal control. The perception of having autonomy – of having control – over the things that happen in our lives, has long been known to increase our wellbeing and cognitive functioning, and to improve our health. Across the globe, psychological prosperity (such as a sense of autonomy), as opposed to economic prosperity, better predicts feelings of wellbeing (Diener, Ng, Harter, & Arora, 2010).

The principle of autonomy is also critical in business and organisations. Workers can be content with only a sense of power, only a sense of control – or both – but having neither power nor control leads to job dissatisfaction and reduced output. These findings have specific implications in facilitation; facilitators should be able to increase the satisfaction of individuals with a relatively powerless or low-level input into the session by giving them a greater perception of choice (through asking them to share their opinion or through promoting the value of their input), thereby increasing autonomy. By instilling a sense of autonomy in all participants, the facilitation will have a greater chance at successfully achieving the agreed-upon outcomes and solutions.

Social neuroscience research highlights the cognitive and neural mechanisms underlying this phenomenon – since the perception of autonomy is processed in the brain as a reward (and that fostering intrinsic motivation is also rewarding), implementing facilitator practices that increase autonomy and intrinsic motivation in participants will increase productivity and promote collaboration among the members of the session.

Leaders can give people autonomy very simply by allowing people to make choices wherever they can, such as flexibility in work design – in the "how to" of projects – instead of explicitly explaining how to do things. Even when it comes to a performance review, giving someone a choice of time or venue may reduce the threat response.

Relatedness (Bonding)

Our evolutionary wiring predisposes us to be social. We can't do without food, water, shelter and social connection. Mammals are born immature relative to most other animals. Fundamental needs not being met cause pain. Social disconnection activates the brain's pain circuitry and causes social pain, which on brain scans shows up in the same area as physical pain. The pain of rejection or exclusion is as real as physical pain and our language reflects that – hurt feelings, broken heart, gutted!

To minimise pain and maximise reward, as leaders, taking a genuine interest in your people, in who they are, their goals and dreams, increases empathy and understanding.

When faced with an in-group and an out-group under your leadership, failure to address such a situation has consequences beyond productivity. As one executive once told a McKinsey consultant, "I have never fired an engineer for bad engineering, but I have fired an engineer for lack of teamwork." Fail to appreciate the social impact of change on the individual and team and expect disengagement and disciplinary issues.

The degree to which people feel a sense of connectedness and similarity to those around them is directly related to whether or not people feel they are engaging in safe or threatening social interactions. Relatedness isn't just about feeling good. The phenomena known as *in-group preference* and *out-group bias* refer to the consistent finding that people feel greater trust and empathy towards people who are similar to themselves and are part of their same social circles, and greater distrust and reduced empathy towards those who are perceived as dissimilar and members of other social groups.

If two groups (or teams of people) need to work together, fostering more social contact between groups is one way to increase relatedness and decrease a sense of threat. In some facilitations, groups (or individuals) who are at odds with each other (in opinion, in goals, in motivations, etc.) are often required to come together to reach an agreed outcome and solutions.

By identifying and demonstrating a "common ground" upon which the two parties can relate, the facilitator can guide the session towards a favourable outcome.

It should also be noted that the definition of *in-group* and *out-group* members is not limited to racial, ethnic or political distinctions, but that arbitrarily assigning people to different teams can have the same effects of increasing liking for members of one's own team and decreasing liking for members of the other team (Van Bavel, Packer, & Cunningham, 2008).

Mitigating *in-group bias* and *out-group prejudice* is an important consideration when facilitating collaboration among individuals who may perceive outside individuals as a threat (e.g. an independent consultant, a new team of co-workers).

Equity (Fairness)

The perception of the fairness of any situation is not based on "cold", rational thought processes, but instead, emotions are integral to judging fairness, and those judgements emerge over time through social experiences with others (Barsky, Kaplan & Beal, 2011). Even when fair and unfair offers are made equally valuable, people are happier to receive fair offers than unfair ones; receiving fair compared with unfair offers activates reward regions in the brain (Tabibnia, Satpute, & Lieberman, 2008).

Accordingly, increasing the perception of fairness and reducing unfairness will promote satisfaction and wellbeing, especially in social situations in which sensitivity to interpersonal equality and inequality is heightened, such as during a facilitation. Any time a group of individuals is brought together to share ideas – often under additional pressures of time and budget – there exists a potential for a heightened degree of interpersonal inequality (whether real, perceived or otherwise). The facilitator must remain vigilant in recognising, identifying and addressing any issues of inequality that may arise during a facilitation session.

It must be remembered that not only the receiving but also the making of fair offers activates reward and "'theory of mind" related brain regions (Weiland, Hewig, Hecht, Mussel, & Miltner, 2012). As detailed in Chapter 4 (in conflict resolution), the principle of fairness is critical in effective and productive social interaction between the participants of the facilitation. The facilitator should always promote fairness in both the receiving of offers and when offers or proposals are made.

The brain requires fairness both in how the "self" is treated and how "others" are treated. The brain quickly puts someone into a threat space if they perceive they are being unfairly treated. It is all about perception, as perception is reality.

The degree of fairness in the authenticity of the facilitator will be reflected in the overall fairness of the outcomes and solutions developed by the participants. Be balanced, consistent, transparent, open, honest and generous.

Reputation (Status)

People are acutely sensitive to their social status – their importance relative to others – and tend to be accurate judges of where they fall on the social ladder (Srivastava & Anderson, 2011). When we actively and consciously consider our status-related information (such as when we compare ourselves with someone more affluent or with a more prestigious job), it affects both our behaviour and threat/reward neural activation. Someone who highly values status may be more likely to react to status-threatening situations in an aggressive and confrontational manner (as sometimes occurs in a facilitation regarding a controversial issue). Threats to – or confirmation of – status influence the way in which people perceive others and interact in social settings.

Giving recognition where it's due, asking for someone's opinion, seeking permission on when to provide feedback, providing opportunities for learning and growth all contribute to meeting this human need and inspiring engagement.

"The acquisition of one's good reputation robustly activated reward-related brain areas, notably the striatum, and these overlapped with the areas activated by monetary rewards" (Izuma, 2008).

There is both a multiplier effect when more than one of these domains are impinged upon, and an offsetting effect when one or more are enhanced to make up for a known deficit in other. "I am wondering whether you would consider becoming a contractor, which means less security, but more money and autonomy."

In a facilitation setting, there will always be participants who are focused on fortifying or defending their status within the group or, more broadly, within the organisation. This underlying motivation can be an antagonist towards successfully reaching the agreed-upon outcomes and solutions. The effective facilitator can use his or her understanding of the **status** domain (as part of the CARER model) to anticipate, identify and deal with any status issues.

Be willing to be wrong, open to correction, generous with acknowledgement, strong on developing others, delegate and be flexible. Don't put people down, ignore them, be condescending, aloof, arrogant or impatient.

Dynamic CARER Domain Links

Having familiarised themselves with the individual CARER domains, the facilitator should also be aware that two or more CARER domains can act dynamically, intrinsically linked to particular behavioural patterns.

For example, individuals who experience high levels of anxiety in social situations (social anxiety disorder), perceive themselves as having low social rank (the **status** domain), but also have low perceived closeness with others (the **relatedness** domain), including peers, friends and romantic partners. Put simply, difficulties relating to others are associated with perceptions of reduced social status.

Accordingly, the facilitator should be aware that demonstrated behaviours may be the result of more than one of the CARER domains combining together.

In another example, relating to – and understanding – others, usually involves some degree of uncertainty or ambiguity because we have to guess or deduce what other people are thinking or feeling. Meaning, that both the **certainty** and **relatedness** domains are triggered together. Likewise, people who have a very low tolerance for ambiguity, exhibit higher levels of race- and gender-based prejudice (Roets & Van Hiel, 2011).

By clearly understanding how the individual CARER domains exhibit themselves in human behaviour, the facilitator will be better placed to identify when two or more of these domains link together and relate to one another.

CARER and Facilitation

The difficulties and challenges that facilitations inherently create need to be offset for productive collaboration and successful outcomes and solutions. Successful facilitators do this by increasing relatedness, which can come from identifying and focusing on shared goals, and also by being authentic and open so that people share positive human experiences (George, 2003). Alternatively, a facilitator may increase a sense of certainty through extensive sharing of information or being clear about where people have value and authority, and thus autonomy.

The CARER model provides an intuitive and easily remembered framework for facilitators to conceptualise the main factors that influence the way people perceive and respond to social situations. The five factors of the model – Certainty, Autonomy, Relatedness, Equity and Reputation – all affect the extent to which a person feels threatened or rewarded in social settings, and therefore the extent to which a person is able to collaborate effectively with others in a facilitation (which, at its core, is simply an organisationally geared social situation).

Understanding individual variation can have many benefits. Identifying an individual's CARER attributes can help tailor engagement of each participant by focusing on their key drivers, rather than all domains at once. This kind of assessment can be helpful because of our tendency to think that others perceive the world as we do, a bias called the *false consensus effect* (Ross, Greene & House, 1977; Krueger & Clement, 1994). Without some kind of awareness of other people's motivators, facilitators and peers will tend to try to motivate in the way they themselves would be motivated.

By identifying the participant's behaviour in terms of the CARER paradigm, the facilitator will be able to guide the individual (and subsequently the group as a whole) to more productive participation in the session. For example, a participant who is highly anxious in uncertain situations will likely need more clarity and concrete detail than a person who is more tolerant of uncertainty. The facilitator will be able to shape the social interactions between individual members to create a safe environment, thus promoting individual reward and increasing productivity.

Facilitators should understand that they are under constant, social magnification; everyone is watching them, looking for meaning and even subconsciously taking on their emotions. All social interactions for a facilitator are meaningful and must be done with care. This is why it is so important to take advantage of psychology and social neuroscience research and to be aware of implicit or subconscious influences on behaviour, especially social signals and biases. Understanding and internalising the CARER model can help facilitators become more socially sensitive and socially adaptive, helping them to use social rewards and threats in more deliberate, useful ways that are in line with a facilitation's objectives.

CONCLUSIONS

When a number of these five social needs are violated, such as an organisational restructure, there is a multiplier effect in terms of increased threat. This can be mitigated in part by engaging people in the process early and asking for, and taking into account, their input; acknowledging the potential social impact; keeping them up to date and so on. By anticipating the potential CARER impact, a leader can also offset a violation of one or more needs by increasing the fulfilment of another. Although the CARER needs are pretty generic, there will be differences in their individual importance.

In summary, this chapter has hopefully stimulated your thinking and provided some tips to assist you in collaborating, influencing and persuading those you lead in more effective and brain-friendly ways.

Economic theory that purports that individuals are purely rational decision-makers is clearly false; people are also significantly driven by social information and social motivations in the form of both threats and rewards. Facilitators who acknowledge this and take advantage of being able to reduce threat and foster reward in each of the CARER domains are going to be much more successful than those who expect people to suppress their emotions and social needs.

A FACILITATIVE APPROACH TO LEARNING

Types of Facilitation

The Neutral Facilitator

- Is a neutral helper of the group and does not contribute their own ideas opinions nor does he/she evaluate those of the participants.
- Keeps the group focused on the agreed task from start to finish.
- Suggests methods of proceeding or problem-solving techniques.
- Encourages equal participation.
- Helps to protect individuals from personal attack.
- May help to plan and follow up a meeting.
- Has no formal power, but is "quietly authoritative".

The Trainer as a Facilitator

- Plans the process and content of an event.
- Contributes a high degree of their own ideas and opinions.
- Uses facilitative methods to encourage participation and learning.
- Tries not to dominate.
- Often does have some kind of formal authority, especially in the training establishment.

Process versus Content

A content facilitator (trainer) can be the acknowledged content expert in the room and may input large sections of relevant and applicable content, data or information for the group to utilise during their workshop/program (Table 5.6).

TABLE 5.6

Process versus Content

A group is capable of more than any one member thinks.	The role of the facilitator is to tap the energy of the group and help create synergy.
Trust the resources of the group.	The facilitator must have confidence and instil confidence that the group has the skills to work through their chosen process.
Honour each group member.	Members of the group must always be treated as though they are acting with honour and with the best intentions of the group.
Keep the group space safe.	The physical space must be guarded from interruptions and intrusions.
Stand in the group's purpose.	The facilitator must always keep the group on track and keep its purpose front and centre.
Be adaptable.	A facilitator should plan ahead but should be prepared enough to adjust the plan to what is happening at any particular moment.
Work with conflict.	Conflict is natural and should be encouraged to be expressed openly.
Don't be attached to your own interventions.	The only reason to implement a particular intervention is to keep the group focused. If an intervention is not working, abandon it quickly and move on.
Be culturally sensitive.	Knowledge of the group's customs, rituals and sensitivities is key to completing any process.

A content facilitator (trainer) can lead the direction of the group.

Organising "Brainstorming" Information: The ToP Method

Lists are relatively easy to brainstorm either as a plenary group, as small groups or as individuals. What is sometimes more difficult is the organising or "rolling up" lists and "putting similar ideas" together.
When organising lists:

- Keep all the information visible.
- Make the obvious connections or combinations first.
- Don't put information together prematurely if there is some hesitation.
- Anything that does not fit with something else should be left and discussed when the rest of the organising is done.
- Try and avoid naming the categories that emerge until all the items on the list are organised.

- Try to aim for a good spread of information across a range of categories.
- Keep the whole group involved; this might mean getting the group to organise their own items.

A good technique for organising information is to label emerging categories with symbols as opposed to names or titles, such as:

X, +, O, *, #, etc

These can then be referred to as stars or circles instead of titles with meaning. Avoid using numbers or letters, as this implies a ranking order. The symbols should be neutral.

When all the items from a brainstorm or list have been organised then the naming of the categories under the symbols can take place.

The category names will normally emerge from the items that go to make up that category:

- Establish a broad area or arena of the category.
- Determine what aspects make up the category name.
- If someone in the group disagrees with a category name get them to propose an alternative.
- Avoid voting, as this will always divide a group.

Finish the naming by getting everyone to affirm or agree to the category names verbally.

Pyramid Brainstorming

Pyramid brainstorming involves the following process:

- Individuals write down ideas on paper or post-its.
- Then the group doubles up, i.e. individuals become pairs, review ideas, remove duplication and add any new ones.
- Then pairs double up to make fours, same process, review, remove duplication and so on.
- Then first four presents their ideas, second four adds their ideas without adding any duplicates, i.e. only new or different ideas, and then the next group and so on.
- As groups get up to present their ideas, they can also be grouping them with like ideas already out.

The key to this process is ensuring you have the right question to ask to ensure you get the output that you want!

Forced Comparison: Use of Sticky Dots

A forced comparison diagram is a simple but very effective tool to identify, in good time, what the various Drivers and Restrainers are; it is based on the traditional Force Field diagram (Kurt Lewin). This diagram can help identify what would help and what would restrain, so a judgement can be made about the severity of each Driver and Restrainer. It can also be used to assess the overall impact of the combination of Drivers and Restrainers.

The beauty of this diagram lies in its simplicity, which enables anybody to grasp and use the concept in minutes.

Process

The concept is simply that a chart is put up with a vertical line drawn on it. Then call one side Drivers and the other Restrainers or use more appropriate headings. You can also use a prepared list down the left-hand side if this helps your particular session.

List the forces (Drivers) encouraging or helping the change or activity to take place. List the blockers (Restrainers) blocking the change or activity to take place.

The "trick" of using this type of tool is group participation. Ask the group to review your question or list, and then using the sticky dots (different colours) get them to indicate strengths and development needs by sticking their dots on the appropriate place on a flipchart (Table 5.7).

Once completed, review the list, identify commonality and differences and discuss these as appropriate.

TABLE 5.7

Example Flipchart of Capturing Actions

Process – the how	Content – the what
• Methods and procedures.	• Topics for discussion.
• How relations are maintained.	• The task at hand.
• Tools that are used.	• Problems being solved.
• Rules or norms that are set.	• Decisions being made.
• Group dynamics.	• Agenda items.
• Climate/environment.	• Goals and objectives.

You can use this list to then identify any necessary action(s) or strategies to improve.

Basic Tools

Flipcharts

Flipcharts are a very useful tool when facilitating groups and have two key roles:

1. Providing a "group memory".
2. Facilitating the process.

Providing a "Group Memory"

The visible display of what the group has done encourages openness, information sharing and participation. They negate the use of information as power – as everyone can see it and use it when they wish. It also helps you to remember where you are and how you got there.

Facilitating the Process

Creating specific flipcharts can help to keep the process focused and moving. The ones most commonly used for this are:

- Purpose and outcome sheet.
- Agenda sheet.
- Ground rules sheet.
- Car park sheet.
- Action sheet.

"Presentation" Skills: The Use of Colour and Graphics

In the facilitative learning context, being able to present in a clear and simple fashion is **important** because:

- It helps set the tone and mood for the session.
- It makes you look and feel prepared and in control.
- It helps create a conducive ambience/environment.
- It helps provide clarity.
- It aids communication.

Here are some of the things that you might need to consider:

- Pre-prepared flipcharts.
- Agenda, objectives, scope and issues log.
- Handouts.
- Key questions.
- Instructions for the group.
- Others?

It is important that any pre-prepared material:

- Is well-presented.
- Is legible.
- Has not too much on one page.
- Is clear and easily understood (not ambiguous).
- Sets the right tone and creates the right image.
- Perhaps has borders on flipcharts for emphasis.
- Has bullet points where possible.
- Has colour – but only use yellow and orange and other light colours for emphasis or highlighting, as opposed to lots of text.

Most, if not all, of this can be done during your preparation.

What cannot be done up-front is what you capture and record as you "facilitate" a workshop/program. It is also important that these visual recordings of the workshop/program output are legible and easy to read/follow. Flipcharts should be numbered sequentially and placed as such around your workshop room.

Some useful tips and some things that could be practised:

- Writing at speed on a flipchart (and in a straight line).
- Try not filling up a whole piece of paper; leave some space in case you need to add more later.
- Use spacing.
- Use graphics if and where you can.
- Write in UPPER CASE or write in lower case and not joined up. Work out what feels more comfortable and natural to you and try to make your writing legible.
- Use borders on your flipchart.
- Use colour and use light colours for emphasis and highlighting.

Many people think that using graphics means having to draw pictures; this is not necessarily the case, David Sibbet (Grove) outlines a "Group Graphics Model" that incorporates the following types of graphics (Table 5.8).

Summarising and Paraphrasing

To help ensure you are listening and understanding properly it is useful to summarise and paraphrase periodically, both with individuals and groups. This also helps when capturing and recording the key points of a group dialogue. It is what many "new" facilitators find the most difficult. It is the first step to understanding where a group or individual is currently at and is the first step towards analysing and synthesising a dialogue or discussion.

Summarising helps you identify assumptions, similarities and differences, drawing on the multiple and diverse perspectives any group will have.

What most new facilitators find difficult is when to stop the conversation and to summarise what has just been said or gone before. Some leave it too long and then have too much to try to remember and summarise, others do it too much and stop the natural flow of a conversation.

The short answer is there is no right time to step in and summarise. At first, it is probably best to do it more often than not, otherwise you stand to lose key points, agreements and differences and so on.

TABLE 5.8

Group Graphics Model (David Sibbet)

Posters	Differentiate, Single image, Point	Single icon, symbol, theme poster, focal metaphor, task titles, targets
Lists	Lined up, flow	Agenda, to do list, brainstorm, minutes, priority list, actions
Clusters	Spaced, connections, get an angle	Freeform clusters, bubble chart, action steps, threefold models, meta-plan, Venn diagram
Grids	Crossed categories	Fourfold models, calendar, GANTT, storyboard, data charts, responsibility charts
Diagrams	Branching relationships	Org chart, mind map, process map, fishbone, decision tree, system map
Drawings	Metaphors, analogies, stories	Lifeline, process models, game plans, landscape drawings, histo-maps, metaphors
Mandalas	Centring, wholeness	Model, targets, visions, group portrait, context maps, radar diagrams

The indicators to watch for in order to "get in" and summarise are:

- Where there is disagreement.
- Where there is some agreement or consensus among the group.
- Where you think the group might be straying off the subject matter.
- When you want to capture or record the group's output, assumptions, constraints or risks.
- When the group starts to go round and round, repeating but maybe using different words or even using the same words (the conversation is in a loop and going nowhere).
- Where there appears to be an "ah-ha" moment.
- When a group seems to have come to some conclusion or has gone quiet (careful about filling the silence too quickly though).

Paraphrasing and Clarifying

Paraphrasing is most often used for clarification. It involves repeating what people say to clarify ideas (e.g. "Are you saying …?", "Am I understanding you to mean …?").

It can also be used to make sure people know that they are being heard and to let others hear their points a second time.

Questioning

It is essential that you think about and plan your key questions and contingency questions as part of your workshop/program preparation and build them into your session plan.

Good questions test assumptions, will invite participation from the group and individuals, gather information and help probe for those hidden points.

A good question (Type A question) will draw out "data", but an excellent question (Type B question) will draw out much richer "data". A Type B question makes participants think of a specific time/place/incident and draws on that experience, examples are laid out below:

Type A = "Can you list the most important characteristics of an effective sponsor?"

Type B = "Think back to a change program/project you were involved in where the sponsor was particularly effective. What was it that you saw them do, heard them say, what things did they do, what actions or activity did they put in place, how did they act around the pro-gram/project team? Now, based on that experience, list the most important characteristics that the effective sponsor displayed."

The structuring of questions is a core skill. Using them in a structured way will help to draw out the relevant data and information you need to elicit.

It is good practice to have your key questions written up on flipcharts for the group to see so you do not have to keep repeating them and so the group can refer to them when they need to.

Below is a structured conversation model that utilises different levels of questioning. There are suggested questions, and you might find these questions useful as starters for referring to. This model is based on the Institute of Cultural Affairs (ICA) Technology of Participation (ToP) focused conversation model, **ORID**. This model uses four levels of questioning:

- **O**bjective – questions about "getting the facts" (**FACTS**).
- **R**eflective – questions about "getting to the personal reactions, emotions, feelings and associations" (**FEELINGS**).
- **I**nterpretive – questions to draw out "meaning, values, significance" (**IMPLICATIONS**).
- **D**ecisional – questions to identify "future resolves, resolution, what are we going to do about this?" (**DECISIONS**).

The **ORID** model is ordered so that a progression of consciousness occurs, with a structure for effective communication using a series of questions that follows a natural thinking process.

Multiple Learning Styles

Multiple learning styles – the way we think and learn (Table 5.9):

- We have all 8.
- Intelligence can be taught.
- Everyone has a strength.
- Everyone has a weakness.
- Weaknesses can be strengthened.
- Each brain is unique as a fingerprint.

TABLE 5.9

Multiple Learning Styles

Objective questions	Reflective questions
• What are some of the activities or initiatives that are currently taking place? • Who are the people involved? • What problems are they trying to solve? • What are some of the policies? • What is the one initiative we have recently been asked to implement?	• What has been the past experience of this group or company in trying to address these issues? • What has prevented this from happening? • What was working before? • How do you feel about this new policy? • What do you like or dislike? • Which bits were you most pleased with?
Interpretive questions	Decisional questions
• Why were these initiatives successful? • What lessons can be learned? • How might we overcome some of these problems? • What coordination or activity is required? • What is the effect of? • How will it make a difference to the way we do our work? • What will the implications be? • What might we have done differently?	• What needs special attention? • What can we do to make sure this doesn't happen again? • What are some of the first steps we need to take? • When do we need to review? • Who will make sure this happens? • What can we do in the future?

Based on the ORID Focused Conversation Model – ToP ICA.

CHAPTER SUMMARY

The key points of this chapter are to understand:

- Facilitating a synergistic dynamic
- The dimensions of group interactions and relationships and introduction to the seven dimensions of relationships in the group setting, including physical, cognitive, emotional, energy, intuitive, strategic and synergistic.
- The application of the Tuckman model of the cyclic nature of group dynamics and how to move them through each phase.
- How to deal with different personality types and leverage their strengths for the benefit of the group outcome.
- The basics of neuroscience of why this happens helps the master facilitator become more successful.

6

Special Facilitation Techniques

FACILITATING EXECUTIVE TEAMS

Fundamentally, facilitating executive teams is no different than any other facilitation. The key to remember is that executives are just people too. However, inevitably, the facilitator may feel added pressure, especially if he or she is not a member of the executive team themselves.

Moreover, there may be an increased sense of competitiveness and drive within certain factions of the team – whether individual or as a collective – to push their side of the agenda. The facilitator must have sensitivity to recognise how difficult it may be for people who have seen themselves as "enemies" to come into the same room and discuss an issue.

Executives tend to be under a great deal of strain – time, budget, expectation – and they will have formed preconceived ideas about how they want the facilitation to proceed. The key is to trust your abilities as a facilitator and stick to the methods and principles that have worked for you in previous facilitations, as outlined in this book. You must remain authentic and stick to your strengths and style.

The pressure of facilitating executive teams can be a significant adversary of some facilitators and can doom them to failure before the sessions have begun. Some common pitfalls to avoid are:

- Being terrified of the executives at the facilitation and going in expecting it to be confrontational instead of a collaboration.
- Not doing enough homework in advance — who's going to be in the room, what are their hidden agendas, etc.?

- Not being outcome-focused and driving the session forwards. This leads to distraction and a *"you're wasting my time"* mentality. Next thing you know, the executive in the front row is checking his e-mail, or worse, just left the room.
- Bad attitudes. Maybe your personal feelings are getting the better of you and you feel that the executives sitting in front of you "just won't get it" or maybe you're just looking at your slice of the pie and not realising the 360-degree picture that the executives sitting in front of you have.

The best way to make sure your good facilitation doesn't go bad is to keep your energy up, be excited about what's going on and energise the discussion. Don't just do your homework on the topic of the presentation, do your homework on the people in the room.

The following are some key points to remember when planning and running a facilitation with executive teams.

Overall Approach and Attitude

The instinctive reaction to the prospect of controversy is to "duck for cover". Panic sets in. Typically, facilitators begin a frantic search for methods to prevent, control or even stifle dissent. The underlying premise is controversy and heated debate will hurt and damage the organisation – *and the facilitator's reputation.*

In fact, there is nothing inherently wrong with a heated debate. Moreover, attempts to control and stifle dissent can backfire and may harm the organisation more than a full and open debate. On the other hand, a well-managed debate, in which members are free to speak as passionately as they wish – but within a given structure overseen by the facilitator – offers long-term benefits. It has the potential of starting a process of healing and reconciliation for a divided and dysfunctional issue, workflow or organisation.

Note the keywords referring to debate are "well-managed". Without effective leadership (which is the role of the facilitator), contentious sessions can perpetuate their bad reputation and deteriorate into shouting matches. The resulting chaos and confusion can cause anything from reduced success in the agreed outcomes, to damaging news headlines or even costly lawsuits.

An effective facilitator of executive teams starts with establishing the tone and guidelines for the session, communicating them to the members and gaining their support towards having a fair, inclusive and productive session. The best time to establish the tone and discussion guidelines for a session is at the very beginning.

Establishing the Right Tone for the Session

The more contentious the issues, the more essential it is to set the right tone for the session from the start. The goal should be to establish a collaborative climate, where narrow interests are secondary to the broad organisational interests, where people are treated with civility, dignity and respect (regardless of how objectionable their points of view may be to some), where passionate advocacy is balanced by genuine listening and where discussions are focused on issues and not personalities.

Here is a sample opening to establish the tone for the session:

> Good evening members and colleagues and welcome to this facilitation session. As part of my opening remarks, I need to make some comments that will hopefully set the right tone for this meeting.
>
> As your facilitator, I am very mindful of the fact that some of the issues to be discussed in this session are difficult and controversial, and have challenged and, at times, even divided, the organisation. No one should minimise or trivialise the significance of the disputes that we will encounter. These issues have had serious negative impacts on the organisation's ability to remain focused on its mandate and serve its members and stakeholders.
>
> Clearly, we need to have these issues resolved, and this session is our golden opportunity to do so. We need to debate the issues openly and fully, and hopefully start the process of healing and reconciliation. We owe a duty to all members that we serve to look beyond our past hurts, animosities and personal resentments, and look after the organisation as a whole. Here are four principles that I believe will help us establish the right tone for this meeting:
>
> - First is the principle of **decorum**. We can debate the issues as passionately as we want, but we must focus on the issues and not the personalities. We can be hard on the issues, but we must be soft on the people.
> - Second is the principle of **collaboration**. We need to work together and not against one another. We should be changing our mindsets from adversarial, where it is "you against me", to collaborative, where it is "you and me against the problem".
> - Third is the principle of **listening** and maintaining an open mind. Surely, each one of us has some strongly held opinions to share. But if

we don't listen to one another, we won't be able to discover the bigger truth on which good consensus can be built. As someone once said: "We were given two ears and one mouth, so we should be listening at least twice as much as we speak."

- Lastly, we need to consider the organisation's mission statement, which is to **serve** our members and stakeholders by _____. As we go through our discussions, I would urge each one of you to consider our members and stakeholders and the best way we might serve them at this session. Imagine them viewing this meeting on a video screen and ask yourself: Would they be proud of us and of how we conduct ourselves today?

What I just stated are four common-sense principles: decorum, collaboration, listening and service to our members and stakeholders. I know these principles can help us have a productive and well-focused session. But there is one problem: I cannot make these principles work on my own. I need your support and cooperation. Can I count on you to help me in running a principle-based meeting? Thank you.

Establishing the above principles at the start of the session will enable the facilitator to intervene later in the session. For example: "*Do you remember the principle of decorum that was mentioned at the start of this meeting? Can I ask you to focus on the issues, but show respect to the person?*"

Establishing Discussion Guidelines

It is often said: "If you don't know where you're going, any road will take you there." This phrase must be the unofficial motto for a poor meeting facilitator. If meeting guidelines are not established, how can anyone be expected to follow them? Inadequate guidelines make it frustrating for everyone and can worsen conflict and animosity. Without good guidelines, your democracy can easily turn into anarchy.

Strategic Alignment

At your executive team's retreat or strategic meeting, your greatest challenge – and your greatest responsibility – is attaining agreement on what's most important to your organisation. Strategic alignment at the executive level is critical.

Strategic alignment among executive team members is crucial to:

- Improve an executive team's effectiveness, particularly in making decisions that support the most important, agreed-upon strategies and goals.

- Provide greater clarity and focus on the vision, mission, strategies and goals, and drive the ability to clearly and consistently communicate these throughout the organisation.
- Allow leaders and team members to more quickly and easily make decisions and take action to reach important goals in alignment with what is most important to accomplish.

Without strategic alignment, companies often suffer the following symptoms:

- Not enough trust, collaboration or agreement within the executive team.
- Lack of agreement on the most important strategies and goals.
- Silo thinking and functioning.
- Poor execution of strategies.
- Strategic planning fails to align the organisation to achieve its goals.
- Failure to achieve important goals.

Maximise Your Executive Team's Capabilities

While facilitating executive teams, it is crucial to leverage from the participants their best talents, skills, and capabilities, which will multiply their effectiveness – and maximise their success.

To help you maximise your success:

- Distinguish what you do that works – and do more of that.
- Distinguish what you do that does not work – and do less of that.

Yes, it's simple and common sense. Yet the real key to success is making the distinction: *What do you do that works? What does not work?*

How clear are you about these?

Embracing this distinction can produce profound shifts in your ability to recognise established patterns of behaviour – and your ability to quickly create successful results. This means you must identify the uplifting, empowering patterns of behaviour that improve the environment for you and your team. Plus, you must identify the patterns that deteriorate your capabilities and those of your people.

Patterns are built on ways of seeing the world – your perspective or mindset – that cause you to react using a habitual set of responses or actions. For example, you may be highly punctual and value this attribute as a sign of respect, focus and appropriate behaviour. When your team members are late (no matter the reason) you are likely to react negatively – perhaps without finding out what caused the delay.

Another example: A manager who does not like hearing bad news or does not appreciate disagreeing opinions may react in an insidious manner. This manager's team members will withhold bad news and share only good news. Therefore, the manager becomes isolated with a severely limited understanding of what is really going on.

How can you become aware of your patterns? By understanding how your thoughts drive your choices – and your actions.

There is a huge difference between thinking things through and consciously choosing a response based on insight and understanding – versus automatically (and predictably) responding to circumstances out of habit. Start by identifying what triggers you.

Ask yourself:

- "Do I consider what I like and don't like or do I consider what is most important?"
- "Do I leap into a well-patterned, comfort-zone response or do I have multiple options for responding?"
- "Do I make judgements about a situation or do I evaluate what is happening?" (For example, using an evaluation approach, you might ask: "What would make this work more effectively? How could this be improved? How can we achieve the full measure of success in this situation?")
- "Am I doing the same thing over and over with no results or do I plan where to go and strategise how to get there?"
- "What makes me effective in the areas where I am highly successful?"

When you answer these questions with clarity, you can identify the empowering, successful patterns you employ – and patterns that do not support your best results. Start observing with greater discernment what instigated your old, limiting patterns and then observe what stimulates your best, most productive responses. Done well, the results are profound.

Conclusion

Facilitating executive teams will likely test your skills to the limit. This task will become more manageable if you establish – with the group's support – the right tone and the discussion guidelines for the meeting. Having done this, you will be better equipped to reduce any negative impacts that may arise from any controversy, ego or personal agendas. You may even be able to convert those issues from a problem into an opportunity.

FACILITATING CHANGE

Change Management: The TFDS Model

After facilitating teams through the planning of change management for over 15 years and relating this to findings from neuroscience, I have developed a simple model called **TFDS**:

THINK – FEEL – DO – SAY

Its fundamental core lies in managing people's expectations. Brainstorm the three areas:

- How you want people to think on day one.
- How you want them to feel on day one.
- What you want them to do on day one (what is the minimum they must do).
- What do you want people saying?

Then, summarise those ideas into one or two statements. Once you've identified these key points for day one, then do the same for a later period, say one week or month into the change. Depending on the facilitation, it's okay to pick a period of six weeks or even three months.

The reason this works is in the certainty domain of the CARER model (described earlier). By quantifying the change, it makes the change seem realistic and smaller. You are not expecting people to be able to run a marathon on day one.

An example where this worked was the introduction of a new CRM (Customer Relationship Management) system:

Day One:

Think	NEW – the CRM system is the new system.
Feel	SAFE – the CRM is not scary and I have had some training.
Do	CLICK AN ICON and at least use the system to record a real-life interaction, not everything, just one or two.
Say	This is something that might help

Month One:

Think	THE SYSTEM TO USE – the CRM is critical to capture all customer info.
Feel	IT IS NORMAL – the CRM system is just work as usual.
Do	RECORD ALL – I record all customer interactions to provide a better customer experience in the future.
Say	This is better than is used to be

This strategy puts the brain in a POSITIVE state as it shows respect to individuals, giving them time to get up to speed to use the new system rather than being an expert in the system.

FACILITATING VIRTUAL TEAMS

Anyone who has sat in enough teleconferences has experienced a special kind of meeting hell. The discussion drifts and sags until, to try to get things back on track, the facilitator says, "John, what do you think about the proposed initiative?" Then, after an awkwardly long pause, John responds with: "Oh, sorry, what was the question again?"

Facilitating virtual teams can be extremely challenging. But, when conducted properly, they can be both efficient and effective, even more so than face-to-face meetings. That's right: virtual meetings can be superior to traditional physical ones. The obvious advantage of virtual meetings is that they are a quick, easy and relatively cheap means of getting people together, but there are also other unique benefits that aren't so widely known, including the following:

- Virtual meetings easily lend themselves to being recorded. Many applications like WebEx have a "record" function that will capture not just the conversation but also documents and other materials being presented. So when people miss an important meeting, they can easily catch up by playing the recording. Moreover, some advanced tools enable people to navigate through the recording so that, if they're interested in just a particular section – for example, a discussion about the resolution of a particular issue – they can skip the rest of the facilitation and replay just that portion.
- People can be patched in instantaneously to answer a question or offer their expertise on a particular topic. They don't have to waste

their time sitting through the entire facilitation; they can participate exactly when they're needed no matter where they're located. All this can be done electronically in the blink of an eye, which sure beats the old way of running down the hall to find someone while everyone else sits and waits.

- Participants can easily break off into smaller groups for a quick discussion about a particular topic. This can also be done quickly, thanks to the magic of digital communications. No more wasting time as people wander off looking for another location to chat and then slowly reconvene in the main facilitation room.

But make no mistake: virtual meetings are tricky to facilitate. The primary challenge is keeping everyone engaged. If you're tasked with facilitating a virtual team, the following, brief guidelines should be kept in mind:

Use Video

This is perhaps the most important rule. Not only does the use of video enable people to read each other's reactions and moods, but it also encourages them to pay attention and resist doing their e-mail or otherwise multitasking. Of course, many people will resist video and say, "We've always done our meetings in groups, face-to-face, and it's worked before. Why change?" But now that the cost of videoconferencing is minimal thanks to technologies like Skype, and organisations are spreading their workers spatially across the globe, there's no excuse. In that type of environment, facilitating a virtual team may be the only means to bring people together.

Do a "Take 5"

For the first five minutes of a virtual meeting, everyone should take turns and talk a little about what's going on in their lives, either personally or professionally. This will help "break the ice" and set the right mood for people to listen and connect with one another.

Assign Different Tasks

To help keep people engaged, different individuals could be assigned various tasks, such as whiteboard manager, minute's recorder, Q&A manager and so on. These functions could be rotated for every meeting.

Forbid the Use of the "Mute" Function

A sure-fire way to kill the mood of any virtual meeting is with the dead silence that follows a joke because people have their audio on mute. Perhaps more importantly, mute discourages spontaneous discussion. Of course, if someone is in a noisy environment like an airport terminal, the mute function can help prevent disruptions to the meeting, but those instances should be more the exception than the rule.

Penalise Multitaskers

Without the spatial connection between members (i.e. physically being in the same room) that applies to ordinary facilitations, some facilitators tolerate people who multitask during virtual meetings. After all, aren't those individuals making the most effective use of their time? But the simple truth is that nothing drains the energy from a meeting like multitasking. To discourage it, facilitators should implement a penalty for offenders, but in doing so they should remember that a touch of humour can go a long way in setting the right mood. For example, at one company, a spinning wheel determines a person's punishment, with the needle ending up on anything from small monetary fines to a chore, like cleaning the office coffee pot for a week.

As companies become increasingly global and workers telecommute more and more, facilitating virtual teams has become a daily fact of corporate life. Given that, it's mind-boggling that many organisations do such a poor job of conducting virtual meetings. Just a handful of simple guidelines can change them from awkward and dull to effective and energising. Your job, as the facilitator of virtual teams, is to ensure the meeting runs as smoothly and productively – if not *more* smoothly and *more* productively – than would a more traditional facilitation.

FACILITATING PROJECT IMPROVEMENT

Change in organisations requires resources to produce that change (time, people, funding and supporting methods and tools). Naturally, significant improvements and changes within a business are implemented with project initiatives. But the nature of projects today is shifting as a result of globalisation. Projects are no longer confined to functional area sponsorship or even geographical boundaries.

One of the most fundamental skills of a highly effective leader of projects is the ability to influence without authority across functions, often borrowing individual contributors for projects. Facilitation skills lie at the heart of this ability to influence without authority. Facilitation is a crucial skill for project managers, to be applied throughout the project lifecycle.

Facilitation Skills for Today's Project Leaders

Facilitation enables today's project leaders to engage the right people throughout the project's life to obtain the joint input of business and technology experts at the right time to build the right work deliverables. A skilled project leader should demonstrate the following key facilitation skills.

Inspires a Shared Vision

An effective project leader is often described as having a vision of where to go and the ability to articulate it. Visionaries thrive on change and being able to draw new boundaries. It was once said that a leader is someone who "lifts us up, gives us a reason for being and gives the vision and spirit to change." Visionary leaders enable people to feel they have a real stake in the project. They empower people to experience the vision on their own. "They offer people opportunities to create their own vision, to explore what the vision will mean to their jobs and lives, and to envision their future as part of the vision for the organisation" (Bennis, 1997).

Good Communicator

The ability to communicate with people at all levels is almost always named as the second most important skill by project managers and team members. Project leadership calls for clear communication about goals, responsibility, performance, expectations and feedback. There is a great deal of value placed on openness and directness. The project leader is also the team's link to the larger organisation. The leader must have the ability to effectively negotiate and use persuasion when necessary to ensure the success of the team and project. Through effective communication, project leaders support individual and team achievements by creating explicit guidelines for accomplishing results and for the career advancement of team members.

Integrity

One of the most important things a project leader must remember is that his or her actions, and not words, set the modus operandi for the team. Good leadership demands commitment to, and demonstration of, ethical practices. Creating standards for ethical behaviour for oneself and living by these standards, as well as rewarding those who exemplify these practices, are the responsibilities of project leaders. Leadership motivated by self-interest does not serve the wellbeing of the team.

Leadership based on integrity represents nothing less than a set of values others share, behaviour consistent with values and dedication to honesty with the self and team members. In other words, the leader "walks the talk" and in the process earns trust.

Enthusiasm

Plain and simple, we don't like leaders who are negative – they bring us down. We want leaders with enthusiasm, with a bounce in their step, with a can-do attitude. We want to believe that we are part of an invigorating journey – we want to feel alive. We tend to follow people with a can-do attitude, not those who give us 200 reasons why something can't be done. Enthusiastic leaders are committed to their goals and express this commitment through optimism. Leadership emerges as someone expresses such confident commitment to a project that others want to share his or her optimistic expectations. Enthusiasm is contagious and effective leaders know it.

Empathy

What is the difference between empathy and sympathy? Although the words are similar, they are, in fact, mutually exclusive. According to Norman Paul, in sympathy, the subject is principally absorbed in his or her own feelings as they are projected onto the object and has little concern for the reality and validity of the object's special experience. Empathy, on the other hand, presupposes the existence of the object as a separate individual, entitled to his or her own feelings, ideas and emotional history. As one student so eloquently put it, "It's nice when a project leader acknowledges that we all have a life outside of work."

Competence

Simply put, to enlist in another's cause, we must believe that that person knows what he or she is doing. Leadership competence does not, however, necessarily refer to the project leader's technical abilities in the core technology of the business. As project management continues to be recognised as a field in and of itself, project leaders will be chosen based on their ability to successfully lead others rather than on technical expertise, as in the past. Having a winning track record is the surest way to be considered competent. Expertise in leadership skills is another dimension in competence. The ability to challenge, inspire, enable, model and encourage must be demonstrated if leaders are to be seen as capable and competent.

Ability to Delegate Tasks

Trust is an essential element in the relationship of a project leader and his or her team. You demonstrate your trust in others through your actions – how much you check and control their work, how much you delegate and how much you allow people to participate.

Individuals who are unable to trust other people often fail as leaders and forever remain little more than micro-managers or end up doing all of the work themselves. As one project management student put it, "A good leader is a little lazy." An interesting perspective!

Cool Under Pressure

In a perfect world, projects would be delivered on time, under budget and with no major problems or obstacles to overcome. But we don't live in a perfect world – projects have problems. A leader with a hardy attitude will take these problems in their stride. When leaders encounter a stressful event, they consider it interesting, they feel they can influence the outcome and they see it as an opportunity. "Out of the uncertainty and chaos of change, leaders rise up and articulate a new image of the future that pulls the project together" (Bennis 1997). And remember – never let them see you sweat.

Team-Building Skills

A team builder can best be defined as a strong person who provides the substance that holds the team together in common purpose towards the right objective. In order for a team to progress from a group of strangers to a single cohesive unit, the leader must understand the process and dynamics required for this transformation. He or she must also know the appropriate leadership style to use during each stage of team development. The leader must also have an understanding of the different team players' styles and how to capitalise on each at the proper time for the problem at hand.

Problem-Solving Skills

Although an effective leader is said to share problem-solving responsibilities with the team, we expect our project leaders to have excellent problem-solving skills themselves. They have a "fresh, creative response to here-and-now opportunities," and not much concern about how others have performed them.

———

CHAPTER SUMMARY

The key points of this chapter are to understand:

- The special skills required for facilitating executive teams, defining the overall approach and attitude, maximising your executive team's capabilities.
- The application of the TFDS model in driving the right level of conversation
- The skills around facilitating virtually; this is becoming more and more important skill set for facilitators.
- How to facilitate improvement projects and initiatives.

Section IV

Evaluation and Conclusion

7

Facilitation Skills Evaluation and Improvement

Only he that has travelled the road knows where the holes are deep.

The Futurist (May–June 2012, see www.wfs.org/) encapsulated six megatrends identified by the Georgia Institute of Technology (according to FutureMedia director Renu Kulkarni, see http://gatech.edu/). Each of these megatrends will see breakthrough research and innovation in the years ahead that will affect facilitative leadership.

THE SIX MEGATRENDS

Smart Data that delivers what matters. In an increasingly noisy world, we'll have to sift, filter and be smarter about what matters.

People Platforms that allow people to better customise their social networks. Beyond "true personalisation", people will not just be consumers. They will be socially driven platforms made of algorithms from personal and associated data that they design and tailor themselves.

Content Integrity to monitor our data vulnerabilities and better vet original sources of information. Pervasive mobile devices, sprawling networks, clouds and multi-layered platforms have made it more difficult to detect and address our digital vulnerabilities, drawing us to trusted content sources.

Nimble Media to ease our movement across platforms. Media is evolving from a set of fixed commodities into an energetic, pervasive medium that allows people to navigate across platforms and through different content narratives.

Sixth Sense integrating all our senses in a digital "mixed reality". Extraordinary innovations in mixed reality will change the way we see, hear, taste, touch, smell and make sense of the world – giving us a new and powerful sixth sense.

Collaboration to harness the power of "an increasingly conversational and participatory world".

FACILITATORS WE DREAD

> Leaders aren't born they are made. And they are made just like anything else, through hard work. And that's the price we'll have to pay to achieve that goal, or any goal.

Vince Lombardi

We have all been to workshops or meetings run by poor facilitators. But some facilitators can drive us nuts. When you encounter one of the bad facilitator types listed below, you know you are in for a long day.

The Drill Sergeant

The facilitator who is rigidly stuck on the agenda and puts the clock above content.

The Guardian

The facilitator who makes certain that all conversation goes through him or her and not from participant to participant.

The Know-It-All

The facilitator who always has the answer. The know-it-all can't say, "I don't know."

The Ice Cube

The distant and aloof facilitator who is unwilling to personalise the experience.

The Blabber

The facilitator who loves the sound of his or her own voice.

The Pretender

The facilitator who doesn't ask *real* questions but, only "pretence questions" that are really designed to give the facilitator an excuse to pontificate.

The "I Can't Hear You" Guy

The facilitator who refuses to listen.

The Marathon Man

The facilitator who piles activities on top of one another, doesn't allow for breaks and ignores the need for groups to reflect on a topic or idea.

The Parrot

The facilitator who relentlessly recaps information, restates ideas and summarises the obvious.

The Molasses Man

The facilitator who is painfully slow and doesn't have a feel for pacing, variety or style.

The Passenger

The facilitator who lets people talk too long and gives up the reins of facilitation.

The Storyteller

The facilitator who tells far too many cutesy stories and never really gets to the content.

The Centrepiece

The facilitator who makes himself or herself the real content of the workshop.

The Tunnel Driver

The facilitator who keeps doing the same thing hour after hour.

It is helpful to practise responding to challenging situations by role-playing them with others. As you gain experience as a facilitator you will discover additional responses to these and other situations and will develop your own style.

FACILITATION SKILL LEVELS

> Only he that has travelled the road knows where the holes are deep.

Chinese proverb

Like any role in business – as in life – becoming a skilled facilitator is a fluid process that requires dedication, effort and practice. Ideally, we would all like to develop our facilitator role in a logical fashion – start with a small group and solidly build our way to more adventurous sessions. The reality of many businesses and organisations is that such a preference just isn't feasible sometimes.

Whether at the beginning of a structured facilitator learning process or having been simply thrown in at the deep end, the following are some key skills that will assist you to plan and run a smooth and productive facilitation:

What works?

- Backup – what happens if you cannot facilitate for whatever reason? Have a backup plan or person.
- Allow the planning to get messy – it may feel strange, but it creates a sense of spontaneity. It's not always easy, but instead of micromanaging the process, let it find its own way; "messy" and flexible works with experienced people.
- Know when to call time in the process and when to let it flow. A clock in the room that is visible also helps.
- Get everyone involved; this includes delegation and documentation – include a busy wall of ideas and output, and a "parking lot" for what has been raised, but is out of scope (or time) for the session.
- Have on hand a lot of pens, tape, paper, transparencies, videos, books, magazines, etc.

- Watch body language for "buy-in" and disengagement – some people (often the "reflectors") may need to go away and come back, having thought through the facilitation. Be able to read styles and provide time where needed.
- Remember, if the answer was easy you would not be doing a facilitated session. Also look for the time "hoggers", give them a different task that takes them out of the process from time to time.
- Be prepared to show a little of yourself as a facilitator – you need to get credibility from experience and exposure.
- Never forget that a sense of humour can break ice.
- Have lots of coffee, tea, drinks, sweets, etc. to keep energy levels high. Bring a first-aid kit, just in case.
- Know the culture of the organisation, its taboos and folk stories.
- Remember that a gender mix in breakouts helps, as do different styles.
- If you can get customers involved – great! Utilise both the supporters and the dissatisfied customers, if possible.
- If the facilitation session is scheduled over multiple days, then be prompt with the circulation of documents so that participants have a chance to view them overnight.
- Remember, some people think in words, others in pictures, some aloud and some quiet.
- Energiser activities can be useful but make them quick and quirky.
- Invest heavily in the introduction and in periodic milestones.
- To reiterate, you have to practise facilitation – it's like sport, natural talent only gets you so far.
- Know someone is paying for your time.

The key to an effective facilitation is preparation. Use the above points to prepare your session anticipating possible issues that may arise. Always prepare a "Plan B" and remember that rarely do things go according to plan completely.

SELF-ASSESSMENT

We all operate in two contrasting modes, which might be called open and closed. The open mode is more relaxed, more receptive, more exploratory, more democratic, more playful and more humorous. The closed mode is the tighter, more rigid, more hierarchical, more tunnel-visioned. Most people, unfortunately, spend most of their time in the closed mode. Not that the closed mode cannot be helpful. If you are leaping a ravine, the moment of take-off is a bad time for considering alternative strategies. When you charge the enemy machine-gun post, don't waste energy trying to see the funny side of it. Do it in the "closed" mode. But the moment the action is over, try to return to the "open" mode – to open your mind again to all the feedback from our action that enables us to tell whether the action has been successful, or whether further action is needed to improve on what we have done. In other words, we must return to the open mode, because in that mode we are the most aware, most receptive, most creative and, therefore, at our most intelligent.

The following is an extensive list of questions you can explore to make a self-assessment of how your understanding has progressed through this book:

Trust and Support

- *What did it feel like to have your physical safety entrusted to the group?*
- *What impact does trust in the group have in your work?*
- *What is the relationship between managing risk and establishing a support system?*

Communication

- *What were some of the effective forms of communication that you used in completing this task? Ineffective forms of communication?*
- *How were differences in opinion handled?*
- *In what ways could the group's process of communication be improved to enhance its problem-solving skills?*
- *How could you improve your communication and networking?*

Making Group Decisions

- *How did the group make decisions for completing the tasks during the day?*
- *Were you satisfied with the manner in which the group made decisions?*
- *Were decisions made by one or several individuals?*

- *Did everyone express his or her opinion when a choice was available?*
- *What did you like about the manner in which the group made decisions? What didn't you like?*
- *What ways are effective for this group to make decisions? What are some other ways that have not been tried yet?*

Cooperating

- *What are some specific examples of when the group cooperated during the activity/day?*
- *How did it feel to cooperate?*
- *How did cooperative behaviour lead to the successful completion of the tasks presented during the day?*
- *What are the rewards of cooperating?*
- *What can you personally do to produce a cooperative environment at home or work?*

Teamwork

- *How well do you think you did?*
- *How effective were you in completing the task?*
- *How efficient were you?*
- *How did you develop your plan of action?*
- *What is the relationship between input into the plan and commitment to action?*
- *What were the differences between having a common vision versus not having a vision?*
- *How were relationships handled? How did you pay attention to other people in the group?*

Problem-Solving

- *Have you noticed any patterns in the way you solve problems? Are they productive? Unproductive?*
- *What effect did planning time have on the process?*
- *How well did you execute your plan?*
- *On a scale of 1–10, how committed were you to executing the plan?*
- *What would need to change in order to enhance your problem-solving ability?*

Leadership Roles

- *Who assumed leadership roles during the activity/day?*
- *What were the behaviours that you would describe as demonstrating leadership?*
- *How were individuals showing leadership by supporting the relationships of the team (maintenance function)?*
- *How did the group respond to these leadership behaviours?*
- *When and how did the leadership role change during the activity/day?*
- *Was it difficult to assume a leadership role in this group? Why?*
- *What specific skills do you need to develop to become a more effective leader?*

Giving and Receiving Feedback

- *What are some examples of when you received feedback during the activity/day?*
- *How did it feel?*
- *How did the manner in which the feedback was given make a difference to you?*
- *What are some examples of when you gave feedback during the day?*
- *How did you express appreciation for another during the day?*
- *What are some appreciations that you did not express?*
- *Do you typically express appreciations?*
- *How can you improve your skills in giving and receiving feedback?*

Respecting Personal Differences

- *What are some of the significant differences among group members?*
- *How did these differences strengthen the group as a whole during the day?*
- *What specific instances did being different help or hinder the group from reaching its objectives?*
- *How can you increase your ability to respect and utilise personal differences?*

Closure Questions

- *What did you learn about yourself?*
- *What did you learn about other group members?*

- *What did you do today that you are particularly proud of?*
- *How can you use what you learned today in other situations?*
- *What specific skills are you going to improve?*

Adapted from: Nalder & Luchner (1992) *Processing the Adventure Experience Theory and Practice.*

PARTICIPANT EVALUATION TEMPLATE

1. What factors influenced your decision to attend this workshop?

   _____
   _____
   _____

2. What did you hope to get out of the workshop?

   _____
   _____
   _____

3. What were the best aspects of the workshop that you found most stimulating or useful?

   _____
   _____
   _____
   _____

4. How could the workshop have been improved?

   _____
   _____
   _____

5. What have you learned today that is going to improve your work?

   _____
   _____
   _____
   _____
   _____
   _____

6. How would you rate the facilitation session? (Please circle)
   5 Excellent
   4 Good

3 Average

2 Below Average

1 Poor

7. Were you satisfied with the experience, knowledge and approach of the workshop facilitators?

_____

_____

_____

8. How would you rate the workshop content and structure? (Please circle)

5 Excellent

4 Good

3 Average

2 Below Average

1 Poor

9. Did the workshop cover suitable topics in an effective sequence?

_____

_____

_____

10. How would you rate your opportunity to participate? (Please circle)

5 Excellent

4 Good

3 Average

2 Below Average

1 Poor

11. Were there adequate opportunities for interaction?

_____

_____

_____

12. How would you rate your likelihood of applying the knowledge you have learned? (Please circle)

5 Excellent

4 Good

3 Average

2 Below Average

1 Poor

13. To what extent do you consider you will apply the knowledge acquired in this workshop? How?

_____
_____
_____
_____
_____
_____
_____

14. How would you rate the workshop venue and catering? (Please circle)
    5 Excellent
    4 Good
    3 Average
    2 Below Average
    1 Poor
15. Did the venue and catering meet your expectations? Were your needs met? Please comment.

_____
_____
_____

16. What future workshops would you think would contribute to your development as a community organiser or activist?

_____
_____
_____

17. What support do you need to work more effectively to make change?

_____
_____
_____

18. Any other feedback or comments?

_____
_____
_____
_____
_____
_____
_____
_____
_____

GROUP QUESTIONNAIRE

Adapting questionnaires based on ones from Katrina Shields (1991) *In the Tiger's Mouth: An Empowerment Guide for Social Action*, Millennium Books, Blacktown, pp. 164–165.

1. **Valuing Individuals**

   Are positive feelings expressed and encouragement given to members? (Please circle)

   5 A high degree of positive feedback

   4 A reasonable degree of positive feedback

   3 The feedback was neutral – neither positive nor negative

   2 Little positive feedback

   1 Nothing positive expressed

2. **Clarifying the Tasks**

   How clear is it what needs to be done and by whom? (Please circle)

   5 Very clear description of the tasks and its designates

   4 Good description of tasks and designates, but could be clearer

   3 An average description of tasks and designates

   2 There were some unclear aspects of the tasks and/or designates

   1 Very vague and confusing description of tasks and designates

3. **Expression of Feelings**

   How safe would you feel expressing feelings directly, either about the issue or about people in the group? (Please circle)

   5 Very safe with strong support in a safe environment

   4 Reasonable safe with good support and a reasonable environment

   3 Safe, but with some reservations about support and environment

   2 Reluctant, with reservations about support and environment

   1 Not safe with feelings of no support in an unsafe environment

4. **Listening and Consultation**

   Are people consulted about things that affect them? Are they listened to? (Please circle)

   5 Excellent consultation and excellent listening

   4 Good consultation and reasonable listening

   3 Some consultation and some listening

   2 Poor consultation and poor listening

   1 No consultation and no listening

5. **Respect for Diversity**

Are different perspectives of the class (e.g. age, ethnic, cultural) respected and included? (Please circle)

5 A high degree of diversity and inclusion

4 A good degree of diversity and inclusion

3 Some degree of diversity and inclusion

2 Poor diversity and inclusion

1 No diversity and no inclusion

6. **Awareness of Sensitivities**

In general, is there an awareness of issues such as sexism, ageism, racism, etc.? (Please circle)

5 An excellent degree of awareness

4 A high degree of awareness

3 An average degree of awareness

2 Awareness was lacking in some areas

1 There was no awareness at all

7. **Commitment to Conflict Resolution**

Are conflicts acknowledged and resolved? (Please circle)

5 A high degree of effective acknowledgement and resolution

4 Effectively acknowledged and resolved

3 Handled and reasonably resolved

2 The conflict was identified but not resolved

1 Poorly handled with no resolution

8. **Training**

Is attention given to training and skill development? (Please circle)

5 High-quality opportunities for training and skill development

4 Good opportunities for training and skill development

3 Some opportunities for training and skill development

2 Little attention on training and skill development

1 No opportunities for training and skill development

9. **Visioning**

Does your group create visions together? (Please circle)

5 Effectively and all the time

4 Often

3 Yes, some of the time

2 There are few visions created working together

1 There are no visions created working together

10. **Fun and Humour**

Overall, does your group have fun together? (Please circle):

5 Lots of fun and humour and a great group dynamic

4 There's a good feeling among the group
3 The group is split – some serious, some fun
2 The group is very serious and fun is discouraged
1 The group is morose

After each person responds to all the questions, encourage people to tally their scores (out of 50).

Facilitate discussion about their responses and scores. What insights come up about their organisation and its priorities?

QUESTIONNAIRE: "BURNOUT"

Source: Katrina Shields (1991) *In the Tiger's Mouth: An Empowerment Guide for Social Action*, Millennium Books, Blacktown, pp. 164–165.

1. **Planning and Project Management**
     How clear are your group's goals and priorities? (Please circle)
   5 Crystal clear
   4 Mostly clear
   3 Average
   2 Some confusion
   1 Not clear at all

2. **Expectations**
     How clear it is to each worker (including volunteers) what is expected of her/him? (Please circle)
   5 Crystal clear with total congruence
   4 Clear and congruent
   3 Average
   2 Some confusion and some conflict
   1 Not clear at all and significant conflict

3. **Evaluation**
     How often does your group evaluate what it has achieved? (Please circle)
   5 All the time
   4 Often
   3 Regularly
   2 Sometimes
   1 Hardly ever

4. **Celebrating and Acknowledging Achievements**

How often does your group celebrate successes and achievements? (Please circle)

5 All the time

4 Often

3 Regularly

2 Sometimes

1 Hardly ever

5. **Individual Needs**

How much value does your group put on individual needs and opportunities for development? (Please circle)

5 High value and high priority

4 Good value and good priority

3 Some value and some priority

2 Little value and little priority

1 No value and no priority

6. **Pressure, Tension and Urgency**

What is the overall pace and intensity like? (Please circle)

5 Cool, calm and incomparably relaxed with a comfortable pace

4 Relaxed and steady

3 Neutral intensity with an average pace

2 Some urgency and increased intensity

1 Unrelentingly urgent and intense

7. **Work Conditions**

In general, what are the resources (equipment, venue and wages) like for your group? (Please circle)

5 Excellent

4 Good

3 Average

2 Poor

1 Terrible

8. **General Working Atmosphere**

What is the atmosphere in your workplace? (Please circle)

5 Calm, organised and efficient

4 Mostly relaxed and organised

3 Average atmosphere

2 Feverish and lacking some organisation

1 Chaotic and disorganised

9. **Autonomy**

How satisfied are you with your level of autonomy in your work? (Please circle)

5 Completely satisfied

4 Mostly satisfied

3 Neither satisfied nor dissatisfied

2 Often dissatisfied

1 Completely dissatisfied

10. **Supervision**

How satisfied are you with the quality of supervision you receive? (Please circle)

5 Completely satisfied

4 Mostly satisfied

3 Neither satisfied nor dissatisfied

2 Often dissatisfied

1 Completely dissatisfied

11. **Dealing with Conflict**

How effective is your group at resolving conflict constructively? (Please circle)

5 Highly effective, resulting in constructive resolutions

4 Often effective, resulting in mostly constructive resolutions

3 Sometimes effective, but with unpredictable resolutions

2 Mostly ineffective, rarely resulting in constructive resolutions

1 Totally ineffective, with no constructive resolutions

After each person responds to all the questions, encourage people to tally their scores (out of 55).

Facilitate discussion about their responses and scores. What insights come up about their organisation and its priorities?

QUESTIONNAIRE: "SESSION FEEDBACK"

Presentation Indicators

1. Was the session clearly and engagingly presented? (Please circle)

5 Completely

4 Mostly

3 Adequately

2 Only sometimes

1 Not at all

2. Was the timing and pacing appropriate for the audience? (Please circle)

   5 Completely

   4 Mostly

   3 Adequately

   2 Only sometimes

   1 Not at all

3. Did participants have appropriate opportunities to discuss and participate? (Please circle)

   5 Completely

   4 Mostly

   3 Adequately

   2 Only sometimes

   1 Not at all

4. Were activities relevant and engaging? (Please circle)

   5 Completely

   4 Mostly

   3 Adequately

   2 Only sometimes

   1 Not at all

5. Was there an effective use of visual aids (flipchart, PowerPoint, DVD, diagrams, etc.) employed? (Please circle)

   5 Completely

   4 Mostly

   3 Adequately

   2 Only sometimes

   1 Not at all

Content Indicators

6. Was the content well organised? (Please circle)

   5 Completely

   4 Mostly

   3 Adequately

   2 Only sometimes

   1 Not at all

7. Was the content relevant and useful? (Please circle)

   5 Completely

   4 Mostly

   3 Adequately

   2 Only sometimes

   1 Not at all

8. Was the material clear and appropriate for the audience? (Please circle)

   5 Completely

   4 Mostly

   3 Adequately

   2 Only sometimes

   1 Not at all

9. Was the material supported with helpful examples, definitions and/ or data? (Please circle)

   5 Completely

   4 Mostly

   3 Adequately

   2 Only sometimes

   1 Not at all

IMPACT INDICATORS

10. Was a level of knowledge gained? (Please circle)

    5 Completely

    4 Mostly

    3 Adequately

    2 Only sometimes

    1 Not at all

11. Were anticipated results/goals achieved? (Please circle)

    5 Completely

    4 Mostly

    3 Adequately

    2 Only sometimes

    1 Not at all

12. Will the material be personally helpful? (Please circle)
    5 Completely
    4 Mostly
    3 Adequately
    2 Only sometimes
    1 Not at all
13. Was participation a worthwhile use of your time? (Please circle)
    5 Completely
    4 Mostly
    3 Adequately
    2 Only sometimes
    1 Not at all
14. Did the presentation offer any new, previously unknown, insights and/or knowledge? (Please circle)
    5 Completely
    4 Mostly
    3 Adequately
    2 Only sometimes
    1 Not at all

CHAPTER SUMMARY

This chapter has focused on how to bring facilitation to a strong conclusion and then evaluate you success of the session. The key points are:

- How to evaluate at the end of a live session and then post the session including follow-ups.
- Master facilitators need to become really humble leader and want to learn how to continue to improve.
- Feedback is a gift that we should always say thank you for and continue to challenge ourselves to adapt as our audience develops and changes.

8

Conclusion

I have tried to cover fundamentals, process, listening and questioning, conflict resolution, many models and frameworks, skills, advanced skills and methods. Not all are applicable in every circumstance and part of the facilitator's job is to ascertain what is relevant to the particular group at a particular time. They can be condensed into the key points here. To avoid some common pitfalls, remember these key points:

- Resist temptation to teach, facilitate.
- Resist temptation to answer questions, reflect them back.
- Resist temptation to convince, use questions.
- Resist temptation to sermonise, make the conversation flow.
- Resist temptation to prescribe, help participants to see the bigger picture.

At the beginning of this book, I wrote that to facilitate is sometimes like walking skilfully on rice paper. The group knows you are present, but your footprints are not there. This thought is related to something that was emphasised in the 27th verse of the *Wisdom of the Tao* written 2500 years ago:

> A knower of the truth
>
> Travels without leaving a trace,
>
> Speaks without causing harm,
>
> Gives without keeping an account.
>
> The door he shuts, though having no lock,
>
> Cannot be opened.
>
> The knot he ties, though using no cord,
>
> Cannot be undone.

Bibliography

Argyris, C. (1970). *Intervention theory and method: A behavioural science view*. Reading, Mass.: Addison-Wesley.

Barki, H. and Hartwick, J. (2001). "Interpersonal conflict and its management in information systems." *MIS Quarterly*, 25, 195–228.

Barki, H. and Hartwick, J. (2004), "Conceptualizing The construct of interpersonal conflict", *International Journal of Conflict Management*, 15(3), 216–244.

Barsky, A., Kaplan, S. A., and Beal, D. J. (2011). "Just feelings? The role of affect in the formation of organizational fairness judgments." *Journal of Management*, 37 (1), 248–279.

Bennis, W. (1997). *Learning to lead*. Reading, MA: Addison-Wesley.

Bodine, R. J., Crawford, D. K., and Schrumpf, F. (1996). *Creating the peaceable school: A comprehensive program for teaching conflict resolution*. Champaign, IL: Research Press.

Bodizs, G..(2006). *Rhythms of the brain*. Oxford, UK: Oxford University Press.

Brunt, P. A. (1993). *Studies in Greek history and thought*. Oxford: Clarendon Press.

Bryant, A. (2013). "In head-hunting, big data may not be such a big deal." *The New York Times*. From: http://www.nytimes.com/2013/06/20/business/in-head-hunting-big-data-may-not-be-such-a-big-deal.html?pagewanted=all&_r=0 [Accessed June 19, 2013].

Cahill, L., Gorski, L., and Le, K. (2003). "Enhanced human memory consolidation with postlearning stress: Interaction with the degree of arousal at encoding." *Learning & Memory*, 10, 270–274

Cetron, M. J. and Davies, O. (2008). "Trends shaping tomorrow's world, Part two." *The Futurist*, May–June 2008.

Crowder, R. G. (1976). *Principles of learning and memory*. Mahwah, NJ: Lawrence Erlbaum.

Damasio A. and Geschwind N. (1984). "The neural basis of language." *Annual Review of Neuroscience*. 7: 127–147

Danigelis, A. (2012). "Japanese floating train of the future has arrived." From news.discovery.com.

Davachi, L. and Wagner, A. D. (2002). *Journal of Neurophysiology*, 88, 983–991.

Diener, E., Ng, W., Harter, J., and Arora, R. (2010). "Wealth and happiness across the world: Material prosperity predicts life evaluation, whereas psychosocial prosperity predicts positive feeling." *Journal of Personality and Social Psychology*, 99 (1), 52–61.

George, B. (2003). *Authentic leadership: Rediscovering the secrets of creating lasting value*. Hoboken, NJ: Wiley.

Georgia Institute of Technology (2012). "FutureMedia SM 2012 Outlook." http://www.nxtbook.com/nxtbooks/gtri/2012futuremedia_outlook/index.php#/2.

Goda, Y. and Davis, G. W. (2003). "Mechanisms of synapse assembly and disassembly." *Neuron*.

Gordon, R. J. (2000). "Does the 'new economy' measure up to the great inventions of the past?" *Journal of Economic Perspectives*, 14 (4).

Heath, C. and Heath, D. (2007). *Made to stick: Why some ideas stick and others die.* Random House.

Heron, J. (1999). *The complete facilitators handbook.* London: Kogan.

Honey, P. and Mumford, A. (1992). *The manual of learning styles,* 3rd ed. Maidenhead: Peter Honey.

Honey, P. and Mumford, A. (2000). *The learning styles helper's guide.* Maidenhead: Peter Honey Publications Ltd.

Hunter, D. (2006). *Training for change 2006.* June 4, 2012. From http://www .TrainingForChange.org.

Hunter, D., Bailey, A., and Taylor, B. (1995). *The zen of groups: A handbook for people meeting with a purpose.* Tucson, AZ: Fisher Books, LLC.

International Association of Facilitators. (2000). "Facilitator competencies." *Group Facilitation: A Research and Applications Journal,* 2 (2), Winter.

Ittner, A. F. and Douds, P. L. (1997). *Train the trainer,* 2nd ed. Human Resource Development Press.

Izuma, K. (2008). "Processing of social and monetary rewards in the human striatum." *Neuron,* 58 (2): 284–294.

Izuma, K., Saito, D. N., and Sadato, N. (2008). "Processing of social and monetary rewards in the human striatum." *Neuron,* 58, 284–294.

Jensen, E. (2005). *Teaching with the brain in mind,* Revised 2nd edition (January 1, 2005). Association for Supervision & Curriculum Development.

Karpicke, J. D. and Roediger, H. L. III. (2007). "Repeated retrieval during learning is the key to long-term retention." *Journal of Memory and Language,* 57 (2), 151–162.

Knowles, M. (1984). *The adult learner: A neglected species.* Houston: Gulf Publishing.

Kolb, D. A. (1984). *Experiential learning.* Englewood Cliffs, NJ: Prentice-Hall.

Krueger, J., and Clement, R. W. (1994). "The truly false consensus effect: An ineradicable and egocentric bias in social-perception." *Journal of Personality and Social Psychology,* 67 (4), 596–610.

LeDoux, J.E. (1994). "Emotion, memory, and the brain." *Scientific American,* 270, 50–57.

Lieb, S. (1991). "Principles of adult learning." *VISION,* Fall 1991. Available September 28, 2012 at http://www.ibsa.org.au/Portals/ibsa.org.au/docs/Resources.

Mehrabian, A. (1971). *Silent Messages.* Belmont, CA: Wadsworth.

Litman, L. and Davachi, K.. (2008). "Distributed learning enhances relational memory consolidation." *Learning & Memory.*

Mumford, A. (1994). "Effectiveness in management development." In Mumford, A. (Ed.) *The Gower handbook of management development.* Aldershot: Gower.

Nalder, R. S. and Luchner, J. L. (1992). *Processing the adventure experience: Theory and practice.* Dubueque, Iowa: Kendal/Hunt Publishing Company.

Norman: Parental Empathy. Parenthood, Little, Brown, NY.

Ochsner, K. (2008). "Staying cool under pressure: Insights from social cognitive neuroscience and their implications for self and society." *NeuroLeadership Journal,* 1, 26–32.

Ochsner, K. N. and Schacter, D. L. (2000). "A social cognitive neuroscience approach to emotion and memory." In J. C. Borod (Ed.), *Series in affective science. The neuropsychology of emotion* (p. 163–193). Oxford, UK: Oxford University Press.

Paul, R. W. (1993). *Critical thinking: How to prepare students for a rapidly developing world.* Tomales ,CA: Foundation for Critical Thinking.

Peigneux , P., Laureys, S., Delbeuck, X., Maquet, P. (2001). "Sleeping brain, learning brain. the role of sleep for memory systems." *Neuroreport.*

Poldrack, R.. and Gabrieli, J. D. E. (2001). "Characterizing the neural mechanisms of skill learning and repetition priming: Evidence from mirror reading." *Brain*, 124 (1), 67–82.

Poldrack, R. A., Wagner, A. D., Davachi, L., and Dobbins, I. G. (2008). *Current directions in Psychological Neuroscience*, 17 (2), 112–118.

Reynolds, G. (2005). *Make your next presentation naked*. Available September 28, 2012 at http://presentationzen.blogs.com/presentationzen/2005/10/make_your_next_.html. presentationzen blogs.

Reynolds, G. (2008). *Presentationzen: Simple ideas on presentation design and delivery*. Berkeley: New Riders.

Reynolds G. (2010). *Presentationzen DESIGN: Simple design principles and techniques to enhance your presentation*. Berkeley: New Riders.

Reynolds, G. (2010). *Presentation Zen: Simple ideas on presentation design and delivery*, Berkeley, CA, New Riders.

Reynolds G. (2011). *The naked presenter: Delivering powerful presentations with or without slides*. Berkeley: New Riders.

Rock, D. (2007). *Quiet leadership: Six steps to transforming performance at work*. HarperCollins.

Rock, D. (2008). "SCARF: A brain-based model for collaborating with and influencing others." *Neuroleadership*, 1.

Roets, A. and Van Hiel, A. (2011). "The role of need for closure in essentialist entitativity beliefs and prejudice: An epistemic needs approach to racial categorization." *British Journal of Social Psychology*, 50 (1), 52–73.

Ross, L., Greene, D., and House, P. (1977). "False consensus effect: Egocentric bias in social-perception and attribution processes." *Journal of Experimental Social Psychology*, 13 (3), 279–301.

Schwarz, R. M. (1994). *The skilled facilitator: Practical wisdom for developing effective groups*. San Francisco, CA: Jossey-Bass.

Schwarz, R. M. (2002) *The skilled facilitator: A comprehensive resource for consultants, facilitators, managers, trainers and coaches*, 2nd ed. San Francisco: Jossey-Bass.

Schwarz, R. (2005). "Using facilitative skills in different roles." In R. Schwarz and A. Davidson (Eds.), *The skilled facilitator field book: Tips, tools, and tested methods for consultants, facilitators, managers, trainers, and coaches* (pp. 27–32). San Francisco: Jossey-Bass.

Senge, P. M., Kleiner, A., Roberts, C., and Smith, B. J. (1994). *The fifth discipline field book*. Currency, Doubleday.

Siapas, A. G and Wilson, M.A.. "Coordinated interactions between hippocampal ripples and cortical spindles during slow-wave sleep." *Neuron*, 21 (5).

Srivastava, S. and Anderson, C. (2011). "Accurate when it counts: Perceiving power and status in social groups." In J. L. Smith, W. Ickes, J. Hall, S. D. Hodges, and W. Gardner (Eds.), *Managing interpersonal sensitivity: Knowing when and when not to understand others* (pp. 41–58). Hauppage, NY: Nova Science Publishers.

Stickgold, R.. (1998). "Linking brain and behavior in sleep-dependent learning and memory consolidation." *PNAS*, 99 (26).

Subramaniam, V. N. (2009). "Regulation of iron homeostasis: Is it all in the HBD?" Gastroenterology, 136 (4), 1449–1451.

Tabibnia, G., Satpute, A. B., and Lieberman, M. D. (2008). "The sunny side of fairness: Preference for fairness activates reward circuitry (and disregarding unfairness activates self-control circuitry)." *Psychological Science*, 19 (4), 339–347.

The Futurist (May-June 2012). From http://www.wfs.org/futurist/may-june-2012-vol-46
-no-3/future-scope/six-media-megatrends.

Tambini, A., Ketz, N. and Davach, L. (2010). "Enhanced brain correlations during rest are
related to memory for recent experiences." *Neuron*, 65 (2), 280–290.

Tuckman, B. (1965). "Developmental sequence in small groups." *Psychological Bulletin*,
63, 384–399.

Van Bavel, J. J., Packer, D. J., and Cunningham, W. A. (2008). "The neural substrates of in-
group bias: A functional magnetic resonance imaging investigation." *Psychological
Science*, 19 (11), 1131–1139.

Walker, M. and Stickgold, R. (2006). "Sleep, memory, and plasticity." *Annual Review of
Psychology*, 57 (1): 139–66.

Weiland, S., Hewig, J., Hecht, H., Mussel, P., and Miltner, W. H. (2012). "Neural correlates
of fair behaviour in interpersonal bargaining." *Social Neurosciennce*, 7 (5), 537–551.

Woolley, A. W., Chabris, C. F., Pentland, A., Hashmi, N., and Malone, T. W. (2010).
"Evidence for a collective intelligence factor in the performance of human groups."
Science, 330 (6004), 686–688.

Appendices

APPENDIX 1 FUNCTIONS OF A FACILITATOR

(International Association of Facilitators)

Create Collaborative Client Relationships

- Develop working partnerships.
- Design and customise applications to meet client needs.
- Manage multi-session events effectively.

Plan Appropriate Group Processes

- Select clear methods and processes.
- Prepare time and space to support group processes.

Create and Sustain a Participatory Environment

- Demonstrate effective participatory and interpersonal communication skills.
- Honour and recognise diversity, ensuring inclusiveness.
- Manage group conflict.
- Evoke group creativity.

Guide Group to Appropriate and Useful Outcomes

- Guide group with clear methods and processes.
- Facilitate group self-awareness about its task.
- Guide the group to consensus and desired outcomes.

Build and Maintain Professional Knowledge

- Maintain a base of knowledge.
- Know a range of facilitation methods.
- Maintain professional standing.

Model Positive Professional Attitude

- Practice self-assessment and self-awareness.
- Act with integrity.
- Trust group potential and model neutrality.

APPENDIX 2 LIST OF VERBS FOR CONSTRUCTING LEARNING OUTCOMES AND QUESTIONS*

*Based on Bloom's Taxonomy of Questions as revised by Anderson & Krathwohl (2001).

1. Remember (knowledge):

Choose	Omit	What is the best one?
Describe	Recite	Why?
Define	Recognise	How much?
Identify	Select	When?
Label	State	What does it mean?
List	Who?	Highlighting
Locate	Where?	Rehearsal
Match	Which one?	Memorising
Memorise	What?	Mnemonics
Name	How?	

2. Understand (comprehension):

Classify	Defend	Demonstrate
Distinguish	Explain	Express
Extend	Give an example	Illustrate
Indicate	Interrelate	Interpret
Infer	Judge	Match
Paraphrase	Represent	Restate
Rewrite	Select	Show
Summarise	Tell	Translate
What does this mean?	Which are facts?	State in your own words
Is this the same as …?	Give an example	Select the best definition
State in one word …	Explain what is meant	Condense this paragraph
What part doesn't fit?	This represents …	What would happen if?
Read the graph (table)	What seems to be …?	Explain what is happening
What are they saying?	Is it valid that …?	What expectations are there?
What seems likely?	Key examples	Which statements support?
Show in a graph, table	Elaborate concepts	Paraphrase
Emphasise connections	Summarise	Why does this example …?

3. **Apply:**

Apply	Dramatise
Choose	Explain
Generalise	Judge
Organise	Paint
Prepare	Produce
Select	Show
Sketch	Solve
Use	Authentic situations
Predict what would happen if …	Judge the effects
Indicate how much change there would be	Indicate how, when, where, why
Modelling	Identify the results of …
Indicate what would happen	What would result
Choose the best statements that apply …	Cognitive apprenticeships
Algorithms	Simulations
"Coached" practice	Case studies
Part and whole sequencing	"Mindful" practice – NOT just a "routine" practice

4. **Analyse (breaking down into parts, forms):**

Analyse	Categorise
Compare	Classify
Survey	Subdivide
Select	Point out
Infer	Identify
Distinguish	Differentiate
What is the function of …?	What's fact? Opinion?
Make a distinction	What assumptions …?
What statement is relevant?	What conclusions?
What motive is there?	What does the author believe?
What does the author assume?	State the point of view of …
What inconsistencies, fallacies?	What literary form is used?
What's the relationship between?	What's the main idea? Theme?
What ideas justify the conclusion?	The least essential statements are
What ideas apply?	State the point of view of …
What is the premise?	What persuasive technique?
Models of thinking	Implicit in the statement is …
Challenging assumptions	Retrospective analysis
Reflection through journaling	Decision-making situations
Discussions and other collaborative learning activities	Related to, extraneous to, not applicable

5. Evaluate (according to some set of criteria; state why):

Appraise	Judge
Criticise	Defend
Compare	Find the errors.
Challenging assumptions	Journaling
Debates	Decision-making situations
What fallacies, consistencies, inconsistencies appear?	Discussions and other collaborative learning activities
Which is more important, moral, better, logical, valid, appropriate?	

6. Create (synthesis):

Choose	Combine
Compose	Construct
Originate	Make up
Make	Invent
Hypothesise	Formulate
Do	Develop
Design	Create
Organise	Plan
Debates	Design
Decision-making situations	Reflection through journaling
Challenging assumptions	Modelling
State a rule.	How else would you …?
Solve the following	Propose an alternative
How would you test …?	Tell
Role-play	Produce
Discussions and other collaborative learning activities	

APPENDIX 3 SESSION SCOPE

What's in?	What's out?	What's pending?
➤	✓	☐
➤	✓	☐
➤	✓	☐
➤	✓	☐
➤	✓	☐
➤	✓	☐
➤	✓	☐

APPENDIX 4 PARTICIPANT EVALUATION TEMPLATE

1. What factors influenced your decision to attend this workshop?

   _____

   _____

   _____

   _____

2. What did you hope to get out of the workshop?

   _____

   _____

   _____

   _____

3. What were the best aspects of the workshop that you found most stimulating or useful?

   _____

   _____

   _____

   _____

   _____

   _____

4. How could the workshop have been improved?

   _____

   _____

   _____

5. What have you learned today that is going to improve your work?

   _____

   _____

   _____

   _____

   _____

   _____

   _____

   _____

6. How would you rate the facilitation session? (Please circle)
   5 Excellent
   4 Good
   3 Average

     2 Below Average

     1 Poor

7. Were you satisfied with the experience, knowledge and approach of the workshop facilitators?

     _____

     _____

     _____

     _____

8. How would you rate the workshop content and structure? (Please circle)

     5 Excellent

     4 Good

     3 Average

     2 Below Average

     1 Poor

9. Did the workshop cover suitable topics in an effective sequence?

     _____

     _____

     _____

     _____

10. How would you rate your opportunity to participate? (Please circle)

     5 Excellent

     4 Good

     3 Average

     2 Below Average

     1 Poor

11. Were there adequate opportunities for interaction?

     _____

     _____

     _____

     _____

12. How would you rate your likelihood of applying the knowledge you have learned? (Please circle)

     5 Excellent

     4 Good

     3 Average

     2 Below Average

     1 Poor

13. To what extent do you consider you will apply the knowledge acquired in this workshop? How?

_____
_____

_____
_____

_____
_____

_____
_____

_____
_____

14. How would you rate the workshop venue and catering? (Please circle)
    5 Excellent
    4 Good
    3 Average
    2 Below Average
    1 Poor
15. Did the venue and catering meet your expectations? Were your needs met? Please comment.

_____
_____

_____
_____

16. What future workshops would you think would contribute to your development as a community organiser or activist?

_____
_____

_____
_____

17. What support do you need to work more effectively to make change?

_____
_____

_____
_____

18. Any other feedback or comments?

_____
_____

--- --- --- --- --- --- --- --- --- --- --- --- --- --- --- ---
--- --- --- --- --- ---
--- --- --- --- --- --- --- --- --- --- --- --- --- --- ---
--- --- --- --- --- ---
--- --- --- --- --- --- --- --- --- --- --- --- --- --- ---
--- --- --- --- --- ---
--- --- --- --- --- --- --- --- --- --- --- --- --- --- ---
--- --- --- --- --- ---
--- --- --- --- --- --- --- --- --- --- --- --- --- --- ---
--- --- --- --- --- ---

APPENDIX 5 GROUP QUESTIONNAIRE

Source: Katrina Shields (1991) *In the Tiger's Mouth: An Empowerment Guide for Social Action*, Millennium Books, Blacktown, pp. 164–165.

1. **Valuing Individuals**

   Are positive feelings expressed and encouragement given to members? (Please circle)

   5 A high degree of positive feedback

   4 A reasonable degree of positive feedback

   3 The feedback was neutral – neither positive nor negative

   2 Little positive feedback

   1 Nothing positive expressed

2. **Clarifying the Tasks**

1. How clear is it what needs to be done and by whom? (Please circle)

   5 Very clear description of the tasks and its designates

   4 Good description of tasks and designates, but could be clearer

   3 An average description of tasks and designates

   2 There were some unclear aspects of the tasks and/or designates

   1 Very vague and confusing description of tasks and designates

3. **Expression of Feelings**

   How safe would you feel expressing feelings directly, either about the issue or about people in the group? (Please circle)

   5 Very safe with strong support in a safe environment

   4 Reasonable safe with good support and a reasonable environment

   3 Safe, but with some reservations about support and environment

2 Reluctant, with reservations about support and environment

1 Not safe with feelings of no support in an unsafe environment

4. **Listening and Consultation**

Are people consulted about things that affect them? Are they listened to? (Please circle)

5 Excellent consultation and excellent listening

4 Good consultation and reasonable listening

3 Some consultation and some listening

2 Poor consultation and poor listening

1 No consultation and no listening

5. **Respect for Diversity**

Are different perspectives of the class (e.g. age, ethnic, cultural) respected and included? (Please circle)

5 A high degree of diversity and inclusion

4 A good degree of diversity and inclusion

3 Some degree of diversity and inclusion

2 Poor diversity and inclusion

1 No diversity and no inclusion

6. **Awareness of Sensitivities**

In general, is there an awareness of issues such as sexism, ageism, racism, etc.? (Please circle)

5 An excellent degree of awareness

4 A high degree of awareness

3 An average degree of awareness

2 Awareness was lacking in some areas

1 There was no awareness at all

7. **Commitment to Conflict Resolution**

Are conflicts acknowledged and resolved? (Please circle)

5 A high degree of effective acknowledgement and resolution

4 Effectively acknowledged and resolved

3 Handled and reasonably resolved

2 The conflict was identified but not resolved

1 Poorly handled with no resolution

8. **Training**

Is attention given to training and skill development? (Please circle)

5 High-quality opportunities for training and skill development

4 Good opportunities for training and skill development

3 Some opportunities for training and skill development

2 Little attention on training and skill development

1 No opportunities for training and skill development

9. **Visioning**

Does your group create visions together? (Please circle)

5 Effectively and all the time

4 Often

3 Yes, some of the time

2 There are few visions created working together

1 There are no visions created working together

10. **Fun and Humour**

Overall, does your group have fun together? (Please circle):

5 Lots of fun and humour and a great group dynamic

4 There's a good feeling among the group

3 The group is split – some serious, some fun

2 The group is very serious and fun is discouraged

1 The group is morose

After each person responds to all the questions, encourage people to tally their scores (out of 50).

Facilitate discussion about their responses and scores. What insights arise about their organisation and its priorities?

APPENDIX 6 QUESTIONNAIRE: "BURNOUT"

Source: Katrina Shields (1991) *In the Tiger's Mouth: An Empowerment Guide for Social Action*, Millennium Books, Blacktown, pp. 164–165.

1. **Planning and Project Management**

How clear are your group's goals and priorities? (Please circle)

5 Crystal clear

4 Mostly clear

3 Average

2 Some confusion

1 Not clear at all

2. **Expectations**

How clear is it to each worker (including volunteers) what is expected of her/him? (Please circle)

5 Crystal clear with total congruence

4 Clear and congruent

3 Average

2 Some confusion and some conflict

1 Not clear at all and significant conflict

3. **Evaluation**

How often does your group evaluate what it has achieved? (Please circle)

5 All the time

4 Often

3 Regularly

2 Sometimes

1 Hardly ever

4. **Celebrating and Acknowledging Achievements**

How often does your group celebrate successes and achievements? (Please circle)

5 All the time

4 Often

3 Regularly

2 Sometimes

1 Hardly ever

5. **Individual Needs**

How much value does your group put on individual needs and opportunities for development? (Please circle)

5 High value and high priority

4 Good value and good priority

3 Some value and some priority

2 Little value and little priority

1 No value and no priority

6. **Pressure, Tension and Urgency**

What is the overall pace and intensity like? (Please circle)

5 Cool, calm and incomparably relaxed with a comfortable pace

4 Relaxed and steady

3 Neutral intensity with an average pace

2 Some urgency and increased intensity

1 Unrelentingly urgent and intense

7. **Work Conditions**

In general, what are the resources (equipment, venue, wages) like for your group? (Please circle)

5 Excellent

4 Good

3 Average

2 Poor

1 Terrible

8. **General Working Atmosphere**

What is the atmosphere in your workplace? (Please circle)

5 Calm, organised and efficient

4 Mostly relaxed and organised

3 Average atmosphere

2 Feverish and lacking some organisation

1 Chaotic and disorganised

9. **Autonomy**

How satisfied are you with your level of autonomy in your work? (Please circle)

5 Completely satisfied

4 Mostly satisfied

3 Neither satisfied nor dissatisfied

2 Often dissatisfied

1 Completely dissatisfied

10. **Supervision**

How satisfied are you with the quality of supervision you receive? (Please circle)

5 Completely satisfied

4 Mostly satisfied

3 Neither satisfied nor dissatisfied

2 Often dissatisfied

1 Completely dissatisfied

11. **Dealing with Conflict**

How effective is your group at resolving conflict constructively? (please circle):

5 Highly effective, resulting in constructive resolutions

4 Often effective, resulting in mostly constructive resolutions

3 Sometimes effective, but with unpredictable resolutions

2 Mostly ineffective, rarely resulting in constructive resolutions

1 Totally ineffective, with no constructive resolutions

After each person responds to all the questions, encourage people to tally their scores (out of 55).

Facilitate discussion about their responses and scores. What insights arise about their organisation and its priorities?

APPENDIX 7 QUESTIONNAIRE: "SESSION FEEDBACK"

Presentation Indicators

1. Was the session clearly and engagingly presented? (Please circle)

   5 Completely

   4 Mostly

   3 Adequately

   2 Only sometimes

   1 Not at all

2. Was the timing and pacing appropriate for the audience? (Please circle)

   5 Completely

   4 Mostly

   3 Adequately

   2 Only sometimes

   1 Not at all

3. Did participants have appropriate opportunities to discuss and participate? (Please circle)

   5 Completely

   4 Mostly

   3 Adequately

   2 Only sometimes

   1 Not at all

4. Were activities relevant and engaging? (Please circle)

   5 Completely

   4 Mostly

   3 Adequately

   2 Only sometimes

   1 Not at all

5. Was there an effective use of visual aids (flipchart, PowerPoint, DVD, diagrams, etc.) employed? (Please circle)

   5 Completely

   4 Mostly

   3 Adequately

   2 Only sometimes

   1 Not at all

Content Indicators

6. Was the content well organised? (Please circle)

   5 Completely

   4 Mostly

   3 Adequately

   2 Only sometimes

   1 Not at all

7. Was the content relevant and useful? (Please circle)

   5 Completely

   4 Mostly

   3 Adequately

   2 Only sometimes

   1 Not at all

8. Was the material clear and appropriate for the audience? (Please circle)

   5 Completely

   4 Mostly

   3 Adequately

   2 Only sometimes

   1 Not at all

9. Was the material supported with helpful examples, definitions and/ or data? (Please circle)

   5 Completely

   4 Mostly

   3 Adequately

   2 Only sometimes

   1 Not at all

Impact Indicators

10. Was a level of knowledge gained? (Please circle)

    5 Completely

    4 Mostly

    3 Adequately

    2 Only sometimes

    1 Not at all

11. Were anticipated results/goals achieved? (Please circle)

    5 Completely

    4 Mostly

3 Adequately

2 Only sometimes

1 Not at all

12. Will the material be personally helpful? (Please circle)

5 Completely

4 Mostly

3 Adequately

2 Only sometimes

1 Not at all

13. Was participation a worthwhile use of your time? (Please circle)

5 Completely

4 Mostly

3 Adequately

2 Only sometimes

1 Not at all

14. Did the presentation offer any new, previously unknown, insights and/or knowledge? (Please circle)

5 Completely

4 Mostly

3 Adequately

2 Only sometimes

1 Not at all

APPENDIX 8 TIPS FOR ONLINE FACILITATING

Preparation

1. **Establish clear goals and expectations at the outset**. Make clear to participants exactly what you expect from them. You and your team should come to a consensus on what your basic requirements will be. If your participants will be evaluated or graded, make sure that they thoroughly understand the criteria that will be used. You may want to post a weekly checklist in your announcement of each topic or monitor participants' contributions in course statistics and privately remind them if they are not actively contributing to the discussion.

2. **Provide behind-the-scenes support via email**. Email is a good way to respond to individual problems or to motivate people to participate without embarrassing them. You will want to be in regular email

contact with your participants, either by group or individual communication. If participants send you interesting content-related comments via email, encourage them to post these thoughts to the discussion forum as well. If you receive a number of questions by email, you may want to consider posting a special discussion forum for questions or suggestions. This way everyone can benefit from answers to questions of general interest.

3. **Make everyone feel welcome and heard; create a comfortable environment**. Respond publicly to initial introductions in a way that uses them as a springboard for discussion, connecting participants' experiences to the content and raising questions for consideration. After everyone is comfortable, responses can become more global: instead of responding to each message individually, you can post replies responding to issues raised in several messages. Encourage participants to actively join in the orientation session and to get to know one another. Show your personality so that your participants feel as if they know you. Use an informal and friendly tone in your messages. You may also want to include emoticons, or "smileys", short sequences of letters and symbols that are used to emulate emotions and to express the message spirit.

4. **Foster communication between participants**. Phrase your discussion contributions in ways that will encourage further responses from participants and draw connections between participants' comments. Try to avoid "over-facilitating". You don't need to answer every question and settle every point! You may want to wait a day or two before you address comments to give participants an opportunity to respond to one another. When you do post messages, try to push the discussion forward by raising additional questions.

5. **Model participation and discussion techniques for participants**. Pay attention to the tone of the messages that you post, as you will be setting the tone. Try to be both professional and informal, establishing an environment of mutual respect and comfort while avoiding any sense of intimidation. Being inclusive and making connections between participants' comments will model this type of discussion behaviour and attitude for your participants as well.

6. **Keep the discussion alive; prevent stagnancy**. Periodically post "acknowledgement" messages to participants' comments, even if you don't have anything elaborate to contribute on that point. A simple "interesting idea", "good example," "I agree" or a similar message can provide the online equivalent of eye contact and a nod of the head:

it lets the communicator know that someone is paying attention. Often, this is also a good time to refocus the discussion by posing a new question that stems from the current conversations. Be aware of time. Participants don't tend to check the discussion board as frequently as facilitators do, so part of your role is to make sure the discussion lulls don't last too long. If you keep the discussion alive and stimulating, your participants will have an incentive to check more frequently. At a minimum, you should be reading and contributing to the discussion at least every other day, more often if possible, especially if you have an active group.

7. **Keep the discussion on-topic**. Keep the majority of communication in the public forum, even if you find that some participants prefer to share their thoughts with you via email. Do not dilute the discussions on the discussion board with too much private one-on-one communication. Keep the discussions on track; rein in long digressions; push people forward on the topic. If comments drift off-topic, be creative. Use subtle or humorous messages, or perhaps a humorous graphic or photo, to redirect the discussion. Send personal emails if necessary.

8. **Guide participants through the agenda**. Send out email messages to all participants to announce each new topic, introduce the next assignment and remind participants of upcoming due dates for activities. This can also be a good opportunity to tie readings, activities and discussion questions together for participants.

9. **Make notes of action and parking lot items**. It is valuable to provide a list of action items that can be shared at any time.

10. **Bring closure to each topic before moving on**. It is valuable to provide "we are all together" moments to segue from one workshop session or course assignment to the next. These pauses help to keep the participants united as they establish a collective understanding of what they have completed and what they are about to do. Topic summaries provide this closure in part, but a number of other types of activities can be used to provide these synergistic moments.

11. **Bring session to a close**. It is valuable to provide a summary of the session, the decisions made, action items and who is accountable and when they have to be delivered.

12. **Follow-up with email**. It is valuable to summarise again all the key items of the session, purpose of meeting, outcomes and actions, thanking people for their participation.

Online facilitators should think about:

- Previous sessions.
- Welcoming instructions.
- Reviewing any feedback that is available from previous versions of the course and asking questions such as:
- What were the pressure points for participants?
- Were there clear instructions on access?
- How to welcome participants into the course?
- Were sources of help and information easy to find?
- All navigation and other links (particularly external URLs) should also be checked before the course begins.

1. Plan carefully and thoroughly.
   - Formative activities can include small quizzes which are clearly marked as "practice" activities and are non-threatening. Don't skimp on the feedback; it is not just another chore when composing the quiz. "Good job", "Well done" and "Try harder" are all equally unhelpful.
   - Online facilitators are encouraged to construct their own checklists for a course. A communication plan constructed before the course starts helps you remember what to do and when to do it.

When	Facilitator
Pre-prepared for session	Facilitator brief video or text introduction. About me brief video or text about the session, what to expect.
Pre-prepared start of course	Welcome message – introduction forums. Facilitator leads with first posting and welcomes individual participants as they arrive and post. Encouraging and energetic.
Start of session	Overview – what's up next, where to find background information, action list, etc.; what are the deadlines etc.
Follow-up	Provide additional context, identify aspects of the supporting documentation/data/etc. Where help is if a participant gets stuck.
Every day	Monitor engagement – use session statistics and logs. Read discussion but don't respond to every post (allow participant voices). Be available.
End of session/ week reminders	End of session reminder of what has happened during the week and this leads onto the next week. Remind participants of activities, deliverables, logs, etc.

2. Use a model.

- A model is a way of seeing the world. Gilly Salmon's model is a "scaffolding" model. It helps facilitators to know and to plan what they should be doing as a course develops over time. The model shows the development of the facilitator role; first, a lot of technical support and motivation via welcoming messages is needed.

- As the session develops, the participants become less dependent upon the online facilitator and more engaged with each other. Therefore, group work is going to be much more effective at later stages than earlier stages. Most of the "heavy lifting" will be done during stages 3 and 4.

3. Use icebreakers.

- The aim of icebreakers is to reduce anxiety and promote interactions. Getting to know people is important in reducing anxiety. You can have activities that are completely unrelated to the course material (stranded on desert islands, favourite food/ colour/music, magic wands, etc.) which promote the fun element.

- You can also relate to expectations to discover what these are and make this a group activity. In face-to-face workshops, you may have participants introduce each other; you can do this online too. If you can do some of these and relate them to the course content, I personally feel that that is a good approach. As a facilitator, you get a feel for what people expect and maybe what they already know.

4. Pay attention to participant motivation.

- In order to motivate and engage the learners, you need to know why they are attending the session. Another use for an icebreaker: Were they made to or did they volunteer? This can obviously have a tremendous effect. Give them good reasons to participate; if they are bored or unmotivated, be aware that they might be negative in their dealings with others and be prepared to email them privately. Otherwise, group work could be affected as well.

- The course should have some good formative activities, some of which are comparatively easy. Your engaged and committed learners might feel that they are too easy, but they won't mind too much, while your more nervous types will be encouraged by success. In some circumstances, a competitive element is useful; leader boards for formative quizzes for example.

5. Use forums – make your expectations clear.
  - Forums can relate to models like Gilly Salmon's too:

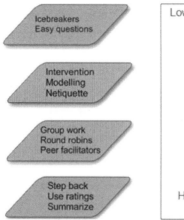 

- They are versatile and have many uses. Not every forum has to have a lively discussion. The purpose of the forums you place in the course should be clear: What's expected of the learners (if anything).
- Finally:
- There are no really hard and fast rules about online courses and their participants; every group is different, something face-to-face facilitators already know. This doesn't mean you can wing it though.
- As well as taking into account the difference between teaching face-to-face and online, be careful that the online facilitation experience doesn't get bogged down by the technology. Every activity, group, individual, blog, wiki and forum should have a clearly defined purpose and not be there just because it can be. Sessions and courses stuffed full of "just-in-case" resources and activities do not encourage and motivate learners.

Index

Accelerated learning, 122
Accommodating strategy, 82
Accommodators, 108, 110
Active listening, 51
Activists, 112, 116
Adaptive, being, 57
Adjourning, 105–106
Adult learning principles, 121–122
    facilitating against, 122–124
    four-quadrant opening, 125–127
Affective questions, 67
After the facilitation (follow-up), 42–43
AGES model, *see* Attention, Generation,
        Emotion and Spacing model
APPLES technique as questioning
        strategy, 65
    affective questions, 67
    focusing/refocusing questions, 68
    managerial and structuring questions, 67
    open and closed questions, 68–69
    rhetorical questions, 67
Argyris, Chris, 73
Asking in the Socratic tradition, 62–65
Assimilators, 108, 109
Attention, Generation, Emotion and
        Spacing (AGES) model, 116–117
    attention, 117–118
    emotions, 119–120
    generation, 118
    spacing, 120–121
Authenticity, 48
Avoidance, 80
Avoiding strategy, 82

Before facilitation sessions, 20–21
Behavioural rules, 32–34
Behavioural techniques in facilitation, 47
    APPLES technique as questioning
        strategy, 65–69
    core values of mastering facilitation,
        48–50
    Ladder of Inference, 71–75
    listening

    art of, 50–53
    to the group, 56–58
    three ways of, 53–56
    questioning, quick tips in, 70
    synergistic questioning, art of, 58–65
Blabber, 171
Blocking, 92
Bloom's taxonomy of questions, 59
    analysis level, 61
    application level, 60–61
    comprehension level, 60
    evaluation level, 61–62
    knowledge level, 60
    synthesis level, 61

CARER model, 133
    autonomy, 136–137
    certainty, 135–136
    dynamic CARER domain links,
        140–141
    equity, 138–139
    and facilitation, 141–142
    relatedness, 137–138
    reputation, 139–140
Centrepiece, 171
Change management, 159–160
Climate and environment, 18
Closed question, 68–69
Closing the discussions, 32
Collaborating strategy, 81
Collaboration, 170
Communication, 163–164
Competence, 165
Competing strategy, 81
Compromising strategy, 81
    accommodating strategy, 82
    avoiding strategy, 82
    consensus decision-making (*see*
        Consensus decision-making)
    negotiation, guidelines for, 82–84
    skilled negotiators, attributes of,
        84–85
Confidence, 48

Conflict
  defined, 78
  dimensions of, 79
  minimising, 34–36
  potential sources of, 78
  resolution, 79
    collaborating strategy, 81
    competing strategy, 81
Consensus decision-making, 85
  agreement and disagreement, 91
    agreement with the proposal, 91
    blocking, 92
    reservations, 91
    standing aside, 91–92
  clear process, 87
  commitment to reaching consensus,
      86–87
  conditions for consensus, 86
  consensus flowchart, 88
  consensus in large groups, 92–93
  decision-making process, 88–90
  developing consensus, 90
  facilitation, 87–88
  guidelines for reaching consensus, 90–91
  key skills for consensus
    active listening, 88
    summarising, 88
    synthesis, 88
  sufficient time, 87
  trust and openness, 87
  working together, 86
Consensus flowchart, 89
Content Integrity, 169
Convergers, 108–110
Conversation, setting the rules of, 23–26
Core values of mastering facilitation, 48
  authenticity, 48
  confidence, 48
  flexibility, 48
  initiating, 49
  integrity, 48
  leadership (presence), 49
  patience/perseverance, 49
  perceptive, 49–50
Culturally sensitive, being, 56–57

Decision-making, 5
  consensus (see Consensus
      decision-making)

Delegating tasks, 165
Dimensions of facilitation
  confronting, 14–15
  feeling, 15
  meaning, 14
  planning, 13–14
  structuring, 15
  valuing, 15–16
Disagreement, 78
Discussion guidelines, establishing, 156
Divergers, 108, 109
Drill sergeant, 170
During the facilitation, 30
  behavioural rules, 32–34
  closing the discussions, 32
  conflicts, minimising, 34–36
  high-level intervention, 38–40
  low-level intervention, 36–37
  medium-level intervention, 38
  non-intervention, 36
  resistance for being facilitated, 31
  time constraints, 31–32
Dynamic CARER domain links, 140–141

Effective facilitator, 48
Empathy, 164–165
Ending the facilitation, 40–42
Engagement, facilitator, 6, 7
Enthusiasm, 164
Equipment, supplies and materials, 18
Escalation, phases of, 32
Executive teams, facilitating, 153
  discussion guidelines, establishing, 156
  establishing the right tone for the
      session, 155–156
  executive team's capabilities,
      maximising, 157–158
  overall approach and attitude, 154–155
  strategic alignment, 156–157
Executive team's capabilities, maximising,
      157–158
Experimental learning, matrix of, 107
External facilitator, 4

Facilitated activities, 6
Facilitative listening, 84
Facilitators we dread, 170–172
Finishing touch, 40
Flexibility, 48

Flipcharts, 147
Focus, levels of, 127–128
    details, 130
    drama, 131–133
    planning, 129–130
    problems, 131
    vision, 129
Focus, maintaining, 57
Focusing/refocusing questions, 68
Follow-up activities, 40–41
Food and refreshments, 19–20
Forced comparison diagram, 146
Forming, 104

Gestures, 24–26
Gilbert, Melody, 27
Goals of facilitation and measures of
    success, 17
Goldberg, Marilee, 58
Group composition, 17
Group conflict, nature of, 77–79
Group development, cycles of, 102
    adjourning, 105–106
    forming, 104
    norming, 104–105
    performing, 105
    storming, 104
Group disrupters and interrupters, 33
Group facilitator, 4
    Schwarz's definition of, 4
Group Graphics Model, 149
Group interactions and relationships, 99
    cognitive dimension, 100
    emotional dimension, 100
    energy dimension, 100–101
    intuitive dimension, 101
    physical dimension, 100
    strategic dimension, 101
    synergistic dimension, 101–102
Group memory, providing, 147
Group questionnaire, 180–182
Guardian, 170
Guide, facilitator as, 9

Hand gestures, 24–26
Honey and Mumford's learning cycle,
    110–111
    activists, 112, 116
    pragmatists, 112, 116
    reflectors, 111, 113
    theorists, 112, 113

IAF, *see* International Association of
    Facilitators
"I can't hear you" guy, 171
Ice cube, 170
Inferential process, 71–75
Information, available, 17–18
Integrity, 48, 164
    Content Integrity, 169
Interest-based negotiation, benefits of,
    82–83
International Association of Facilitators
    (IAF), 8
Intervention
    high-level intervention, 38–40
    low-level intervention, 36–37
    medium-level intervention, 38
    non-intervention, 36
Introducing yourself, 22
Introductions, method of, 22–23

Kissinger, Henry, 5
Know-it-all, 170
Kolb's learning styles, 106, 108, 116
    accommodators, 110
    assimilators, 109
    convergers, 109–110
    divergers, 109

Ladder of Inference, 34, 71–75
Laughter, 29
Leadership (presence), 49
Learning
    accelerated, 122
    adult learning principles, 121–127
    Attention, Generation, Emotion and
        Spacing (AGES) model, 116–121
    experimental learning, matrix of, 107
    frames of focus in learning cycle, 113
    Honey and Mumford's learning cycle,
        110–116
    Kolb's learning styles, 106–110, 116
    multiple learning styles, 151–152
Learning, facilitative approach to, 143
    brainstorming information,
        organising, 144–145
    neutral facilitator, 143

paraphrasing and clarifying, 150
process *vs.* content, 143–144
pyramid brainstorming, 145–147
questioning, 150–152
summarising and paraphrasing,
        149–150
tools, 147
    facilitating the process, 147
    flipcharts, 147
    group memory, providing, 147
    presentation skills, 147–149
trainer as a facilitator, 143
Listening, 53
    active, 51
    facilitative, 84
    to the group, 56–58
    non-verbal, 55
    para-verbal, 55–56
    synergistic (*see* Synergistic listening)
    verbal (*see* Verbal listening)
Location, 18
Logistics and room requirements, 18
Lozanov, Georgi, 122
Luccock, H.E., 97

Managerial and structuring questions, 67
Manner of facilitation, 17
Marathon man, 171
Millikan, Robert, 27
Mirroring, 54
Molasses man, 171
Motivator, facilitator as, 10
Motives, identifying, 26
Multiple learning styles, 151–152
Multitaskers, penalising, 162

Naked facilitator, 48
Negotiation, guidelines for
    create safety, 83
    facilitative listening, 84
    feedback, 84
    interest-based negotiation, benefits
        of, 82–83
    reflection, 84
Neutral, remaining, 5
Neutral facilitator, 143
Nimble Media, 169
Non-verbal listening, 55
Norming, 104–105

Open question, 68–69
"Orming" model, of Tuckman, 102

The Pale Blue Dot, 28
Paraphrasing, 54
    and clarifying, 150
Para-verbal listening, 55–56
Parrot, 171
Participant evaluation template,
        177–179
Participants, four quadrants of, 126
Partner, facilitator as, 8
Passenger, 171
Patience/perseverance, 49
Peacemaker, facilitator as, 9
People Platforms, 169
Performing, 105
Planning the facilitation, 16
    before the facilitation sessions,
        20–21
    climate and environment, 18
    equipment, supplies and materials, 18
    food and refreshments, 19–20
    goals of facilitation and measures of
        success, 17
    group composition, 17
    information, available, 17–18
    location, 18
    logistics and room requirements, 18
    manner of facilitation, 17
Pragmatists, 112, 116
Presentation skills, 147–149
Pressure, cool under, 165
Pretender, 171
Previn, André, 20
Principles governing facilitation, 11
    empathy, 11
    equality, 11
    focus, 11
    free and informed choice, 12
    involvement by all, 12
    mutual trust, 11
    responsibility and commitment, 12
    shared decision-making, 12
Problem-solving skills, 166
Process conflict, 78
Process *vs.* content, 143–144
Program/session, stating the reason
        for, 22

Project improvement, facilitating, 162
    competence, 165
    delegating tasks, 165
    empathy, 164–165
    enthusiasm, 164
    good communicator, 163–164
    integrity, 164
    pressure, cool under, 165
    problem-solving skills, 166
    shared vision, 163
    team-building skills, 166
Project manager, 4
Punch, beginning with, 26
Punch line, starting with, 26
    challenging, 28–29
    humorous, 29–30
    novel, 27–28
    personal, 27
    unexpected, 27

Questioning, 54, 150–152
    quick tips in, 70
Questioning strategy, APPLES
        technique as, 65
    affective questions, 67
    focusing/refocusing questions, 68
    managerial and structuring questions,
        67
    open and closed questions, 68–69
    rhetorical questions, 67
Questions, Bloom's taxonomy of, *see*
        Bloom's taxonomy of
        questions
Quiet authority, facilitator as, 4

Reflecting feeling, 54
Reflectors, 111, 113
Resistance for being facilitated, 31
Responsibilities of facilitator, 8–11
Reynolds, Garr, 26, 47
Rhetorical questions, 67
Roles of facilitator, 5–7

Sagan, Carl, 28
Schwarz's definition of group facilitator, 4
Self-assessment, 173
    closure questions, 176–177
    communication, 174
    cooperating, 175

    giving and receiving feedback, 176
    leadership roles, 176
    making group decisions, 174–175
    problem-solving, 175
    respecting personal differences, 176
    teamwork, 175
    trust and support, 174
Shared vision, 163
Sixth Sense, 170
Skilled facilitator, 5, 172
Skilled negotiators, attributes of,
        84–85
Skill levels, facilitation, 172–173
Skills
    presentation, 147–149
    problem-solving, 166
    team-building, 166
Smart Data, 169
Socratic method, 63, 64
Socratic questions, 63, 64
Starting the facilitation, 22
    beginning with a punch, 26
    conversation, setting the rules of,
        23–26
    introducing yourself, 22
    introductions, making, 22–23
    motives, identifying, 26
    punch line, starting with, 26–30
    stating the reason for the program or
        session, 22
    welcoming and acknowledging
        everyone, 22
Sticky dots, using, 146
Storming, 104
Storyteller, 171
Strategic alignment, 156–157
Strategist, facilitator as, 8, 9
Suggestopedia, principles of, 122
Summarising, 54–55
    and paraphrasing, 149–150
Synergist, facilitator as, 8
Synergistic listening, 57
    active, 51–52
    deliberate, 51
    dynamic, 52–53
    empathetic, 51
    learning experience, 52
    multisensory, 51
    non-judgemental, 52

Synergistic questioning, art of, 58
    asking in the Socratic tradition, 62–65
    Bloom's taxonomy of questions, 59–62
Synergy, 8

Task conflict, 78
Taskmaster, facilitator as, 10
Teach by asking method, 62
Team-building skills, 166
Team leader, 4
TFDS model, 159–160
Theorists, 112, 113
Thoreau, Henry David, 50
Time-boxing strategy, 32
Time constraints, 31–32
ToP method, 144–145
Trainer as a facilitator, 143
Tuckman model, 102, 104
Tunnel driver, 172

Venue, 18
Verbal listening, 53
    mirroring, 54
    paraphrasing, 54
    questioning, 54
    reflecting feeling, 54
    summarising, 54–55
Virtual teams, facilitating, 160
    assigning different tasks, 161
    multitaskers, penalising, 162
    "mute" function, forbidding the
        use of, 162
    "Take 5", doing, 161
    video, using, 161

Welcoming and acknowledging
    everyone, 22
Win–lose situation, 80
Win–win solution, 79–80, 86